Intentional LIVING
· · · · · **THE ANTHOLOGY** · · · · ·

Intentional LIVING
· · · · · THE ANTHOLOGY · · · · ·

Choosing To Win Despite Life's Challenges

Dr. Jatun Dorsey

INTENTIONAL LIVING
Published by Purposely Created Publishing Group™
Copyright © 2018 Jatun Dorsey

All rights reserved.

No part of this book may be reproduced, distributed or transmitted in any form by any means, graphic, electronic, or mechanical, including photocopy, recording, taping, or by any information storage or retrieval system, without permission in writing from the publisher, except in the case of reprints in the context of reviews, quotes, or references.

Printed in the United States of America
ISBN: 978-1-948400-32-9

Special discounts are available on bulk quantity purchases by book clubs, associations and special interest groups. For details email:
sales@publishyourgift.com
or call (888) 949-6228.

For information logon to:
www.PublishYourGift.com

This book is dedicated to aspiring authors. If you have a story in you, let this be an example of your ability to produce. Moreover, let this book serve as an example of how taking the leap to share your story can and will change the world. Someone is waiting on you to show up in order for him or her to break through.

Table of Contents

Acknowledgments 1

Foreword 3

Embrace Your True Worth 7
JaTaun Hawkins

Walking Forward in Faith 19
Patrice Withers-Stephens

Saving a Little for Myself 29
Tiffany D. Hicks

Never Give Up 39
Brigid Roberson

Be Open to Change 49
LaTisha Terry

Navigating the Corporate Majority as a Minority 57
Floyd Dorsey IV

Education Matters 67
Dr. Tara Peters

Awakening Purpose 79
T'Edra Z. Jackson

Don't Fail to Gain Your Fortune 87
Bobby L. Tinnion

Living My Purpose—Finance and Entrepreneurship 97
Kawana L. Marshall

Sources 109

About the Authors 111

Acknowledgments

Thank God for every experience that has brought me to this very point in life. I am beyond appreciative of the responsibility placed on me to influence, encourage, inspire, and empower. It is no easy feat, but one that, if done right, will impact the world and leave a legacy that transcends time.

My greatest extension of gratitude to the coauthors of this anthology, for without all of you this book would not exist. Together we will ensure this book reinforces the amazing talents you have already shown the world—but more importantly we will change the lives of readers who are now struggling with what you have been through. Bless each of you!

Foreword

In early 2017 I released my Amazon best-selling book entitled *Intentional Living: 30 Productivity Principles to Achieve Peace of Mind*. This book laid the foundation and direction not only for my personal life but my business as well. It truly set the tone for how I would continue to approach life and how I would encourage others to do the same. When speaking on intentional living, I often offer this insight: to HAVE intention and to BE intentional are two very different things. To have intention means that you have a plan or thought in place, which is good because that's where all transformation begins. However, to be intentional means to act out the plan. In essence, the latter is when you give life to your plan.

The act of intentional living has released me from some of the toughest spots in life. Divorce, loss of loved ones, business setbacks, career challenges, and more. However, living intentionally also manifested some of the greatest experiences in my life as well. Marriage, good health, business and career successes, overall positive outlook, and the courage to shine bright enough to impact the lives of others.

You see, being intentional does not equate to a free pass from all plans gone wrong. No, it simply means that, before you put one foot in front of the other, you performed the necessary due diligence to ensure the path you take is most likely to return the future or outcome you envision. Without the plan, you fly blind and become reactionary. But you are designed to function as your created self.

That is why I had the vision of publishing a collection of experiences from various individuals who have truly grasped the principle of living intentionally. While in certain life moments they initially were not functioning as their created self but instead as their reactionary self, through their lived experiences they realized the importance of having intention and progressed toward being intentional. In the end, they were able to pass through the challenges that had the potential to defeat the amazing human beings they were meant to be.

In this book collaboration, you will become acquainted with stories of entrepreneurship, education, career, finance, divorce, and personal development—the good, bad, and ugly happenings that broke down these coauthors in order for them to arrive at a breakthrough. You'll find that a common thread is loss; however, as you read for yourself, you'll learn how loss is often a setup and preparation for your increase. You must create capacity in order to receive more, and that capacity might come out of the demise of something or someone you hold dear.

I want these heartfelt chronicles to extend hope, courage, and action to you so that you realize or are reminded of the following:

1. You are not alone!

2. Time is fleeting, and even the storm you are currently experiencing will pass.

3. It is never too late, but neither will there ever be a perfect moment. You must make the moment you have perfect.

4. As with a bow and arrow, there are times when you will need to pull back in order to shoot forward to your destination.

5. Others may doubt you and your abilities, but stand on your confidence and your created being without wavering.

6. How you do one thing is likely how you do everything. Assess all aspects of your life in order to make a lasting change. For instance, if your personal finances are a mess, then your business finances likely will be as well.

7. There are times when you will have to lose before you win again and there are times when you must begin again.

8. If you give too much to one thing, you are not giving enough to something else.

9. You must push past the pain and turn the pain into purpose.

10. Create a plan and consistently work the plan.

May these stories encourage you to HAVE intention and to BE intentional as you go about life functioning as your unapologetic, created self.

Intentionally Yours,
Dr. Jatun Dorsey

Embrace Your True Worth

JaTaun Hawkins

> "Hold my head up high
> I was not built to break
> I didn't know my own strength."
>
> —*Diane Warren*

BUSTED

The phone rang. My cousin said, "Shawn," calling me by my family nickname, "you're gonna be mad. Aunt Frances says you better bring your butt to the house. The whole family's here."

I was busted.

I didn't want anyone to know I'd gone to Queens, New York, or that I was living in my cousin's basement. I didn't want them to know I'd lost my marriage and lost myself. I surely didn't want them to know I'd tried to take a whole bottle of pain pills and spent seventy-two hours in the hospital. I just wanted to be left alone.

But I went. My aunt Frances, the woman who I considered to have helped raise me with great wisdom, laid me across her lap right there in front of all my cousins and had an old-fashioned "come-to-Jesus" moment. I broke down in tears. I was so embarrassed, but she told me, "You hold your head up high. You have nothing to be ashamed of. You never have to hide from family. We will always be here for you."

She put her finger right on the problem: shame. Shame had built me a prison and was holding me back from the very thing that would heal my heart. My family's love and acceptance were waiting for me, but I was so busy hiding that I almost missed it.

MY LOVE

My now ex-husband was my king. He was a Southern gentleman, a romantic, a family man, and my best friend. When my ex-husband and I met at work, I was a struggling single mom engaged to someone else. Unbeknownst to me, I was suffering a tubal pregnancy, and I passed out on the floor in the ladies' room.

My ex-husband heard someone needing help, so he barged right in and scooped me up off the bathroom floor.

Later we laughed about it and I called him my knight in shining armor. You'd think after that, we'd never be embarrassed about anything!

My ex-husband came with a lot of baggage. He has five children, and before we met he'd been married and divorced twice. He wasn't proud of the way he'd handled those relationships, and he had a habit of leaving out details that made him uncomfortable. Case in point: I didn't find out I was wife number three until just before our wedding! I loved him dearly, but I couldn't believe he hadn't been completely honest with me. He broke down and admitted he was scared I wouldn't love him if I'd known about his past.

We got through that moment, but it set a pattern for our whole marriage. He hid what was really going on in his life. I hid what was really going on in my heart.

We were both controlled by shame.

MY SHAME

My ex-husband kept his truth from me because he was ashamed of some of his choices. But my shame went so deep, I was keeping my truth from myself.

You see, I was raped when I was young. My mom wasn't someone you could talk to. When I tried to tell her, she didn't want to hear it. (That's a subject for a whole different book.) On top of the shame that comes with rape, I had the shame of my mother's rejection. I mean, how worthless do you have to be if your own mother doesn't want to help you? That's how worthless I felt.

So, I stopped speaking. If you can't trust people and you're not worth listening to, what's the point of expressing how you feel? I pretty much didn't talk to anyone about anything for years.

My grandmother tried to pull my truth out of me. She'd encourage me to write in a journal: "If you can't talk to people, then you need to write as if you're talking to someone." That helped me cope, but it didn't help me learn to connect. I grew up without any practice in how to communicate or get my emotional needs met.

That lack of communication undermined my marriage. My ex-husband had his own issues, but he did want to know how I felt. He wanted to talk with me. I just couldn't do it. I kept my feelings in, or I'd walk out of the house. Once I tried writing him a long letter, but by that point he was so frustrated he balled it up and threw it away. He said, "When you can talk to me, I'll listen, but don't put me off with letters!" That hurt me so bad. I understand it now, but at the time it was just one more rejection.

> Do you struggle with shame from a trauma in your past? Who did you turn to? How did their reaction make you feel?

- 👉 You deserve to be heard. Do you have trouble communicating your feelings?

- 👉 Be intentional by taking an inventory of emotional or relationship problems that are bothering you. Who can you ask for help?

- 👉 You deserve help and understanding. Do you need to ask for help?

MY BODY

Shame cut me off from my physical health too. I'd always had problems with my menstruation. It was heavy and painful. I'd throw up and have terrible symptoms, but I didn't want to think about my body, and I certainly didn't have the skills to advocate for myself when doctors dismissed me.

By the time my ex-husband proposed, I was menstruating three weeks of every month. I couldn't put up with it anymore, so I scheduled a Pap smear.

You know something's wrong when your doctor starts calling in other doctors to look over his shoulder! That exam turned into a sonogram, and a biopsy, and unending tests. Finally, they told me I had fibroids the size of grapefruits and abnormal cells. Ovarian cancer.

They scheduled me for emergency surgery, and I had a full hysterectomy three months before my wedding.

My doctor prescribed hormone replacement therapy and instructed me how to take it. I don't know if I was still loopy, or if I just didn't want to think about it anymore, but unfortunately, I didn't really get how important those hormones were and why.

My mother and grandmother were already in menopause at that point, and they convinced me that hormone replacement was risky and unnecessary. They weren't totally wrong—for menopause! For a woman my age it was a completely different situation. Instead of doing my own research and making sure to meet my own needs, I just accepted everything they said and never took the hormones.

My wedding was beautiful. I was thrilled to be a newlywed. Nobody knew I had a time bomb ticking in my head—and neither did I.

- 👍 You deserve to spend time and energy on your health! Do you take initiative to get your needs met? Or do you accept whatever you get because it's easier not to think about it?

- 👍 Are you being intentional about the basics of exercise, rest, nutrition, and regular checkups?

- 👍 Are there any health concerns that need your attention? Don't put them off until you can't stand it anymore. Speak up for yourself!

MY WORTH

Like a lot of us, I grew up with fairy tale expectations. A man who really loved me would treat me like a princess. A good, responsible husband would have financial security to provide for all our needs and have enough for luxuries too. I felt like money spent on me proved my value in a relationship. You could say gifts are an important "love language" to me.

Now, all this started with a very sweet, innocent family tradition. My father loved to shower my mother, my sisters, and myself with the best of everything: a beautiful house, cars, treats, and presents, especially on Valentine's Day. Mom got a big candy heart and bunches of flowers. We children got the cheap candy, but plenty of it. It was a big deal. It was my father's way of showing his affection, and my dad is my heart.

As a grownup, I can see the proper proportion here. It was just a few boxes of candy and some flowers, not the Hope diamond. But to a child's eyes, there was a pecking order: the most important person, the person you love best, gets the biggest presents. My dad was doing it right, but children don't always learn the lesson you mean to teach.

My ex-husband had a lot in common with my dad. His love was generous, and he wanted to shower me with affection. To both of us, that meant expensive surprises: trips, the spa, fancy dinners, and extravagant gifts.

Even when the gift wasn't something I wanted, it made me feel special and loved. While we were dating, he had a security system installed at my house without asking me. On one hand, that seemed intrusive. On the other, I knew he wanted to keep me safe. I liked that feeling of being protected and watched over. He replaced my older car with a new red one, and had vanity plates put on that said "MZ JR". I felt funny about it, but with his great credit, I wound up with a smaller payment for a better ride. Again, I silenced my questions and focused on appreciating the gesture.

My ex-husband had a good career when we met, but he made a lot of bad decisions about money. He was supporting children in three different households. As the pressure grew, he started reaching for jobs he wasn't qualified for, which meant he couldn't keep up with the work and couldn't keep the job. His life—our life—became a cycle of work problems, money problems, legal problems, and marriage problems.

> 👍 Are you and your romantic partner acting out scripts you learned in childhood? Try to look at those patterns with your grownup eyes. Do they reflect a childish understanding of love? Be intentional by examining what those gestures of affection mean to you. Write it out in a journal or talk it over with a friend, therapist, or advisor. Do those feelings match the principles and values you live by? Maybe they do—great! If they don't, how can you address that with your partner?

👍 Does your partner do things that feel like overstepping? Would you rather he asked before making decisions that affect you? Be intentional by talking with him about your feelings. Remember, someone who loves you wants to make you happy, not nervous. Someone who loves you wants to know what's deep down in your heart. Honesty isn't rude or ungrateful. It's being real.

BUSTED OUT

My ex-husband was a faithful, nurturing husband to me, and I wanted to be a loving, accepting wife. I figured the difficulties we faced were just "part of the package," and I tried to cope without nagging or complaining. I tried to keep my pain and my needs to myself, but that backfired.

Ignoring my health backfired, too. When I said I lost myself, that wasn't just a colorful metaphor.

My reproductive organs had been removed because of my cancer. They don't just make babies, you know! Every part of your body balances everything else. By not taking the hormone replacements, I was slowly starving my brain of the ability to function properly. I started literally losing my mind.

My emotions were out of control. My coping skills disappeared. Instead of treating my ex-husband with love and kindness, I became resentful, hurtful, and cruel. I treated him with disrespect and contempt.

Our lives became chaotic and unsustainable. The more volatile I got, the more problems my ex-husband tried to hide. The more hidden problems jumped up, the more I came apart. We couldn't even agree on if or when to file divorce papers. Eventually, it was just too late.

When my poor, messed-up body laid me out with kidney stones that led to me needing high-powered pain pills, I was at the end of my rope. I couldn't tell myself any more fairy tales to make things look better. The only place left to hide was in the ground.

Thank God, I failed. Thank God, I had my cousin beside me. And thank God, I got busted and had to go see Aunt Frances.

I thought I was the only woman in my family who'd ever been separated or divorced. I was a failure. An outcast. Instead, my aunts and cousins circled around me and started sharing their stories, their pain, and their road back to themselves.

They didn't bust me, they busted me out of that prison of shame. That day didn't magically make my problems disappear. I still needed doctors, therapists, and a lot of time to rebuild my life. But their truth gave me strength to face my truth. Their love helped me believe I was worth loving. I realized that day that, no matter what, I will always love my ex-husband, but I love JaTaun too!

It's amazing what freedom can do for your heart. In the end, I realized that loving my ex-husband meant wanting what was best for him. I knew he longed to be in his youngest son's life full-time, so I wrote him a long letter and advised him to go back to his second wife.

I hope my story helps you find freedom too. When you know your worth, you can love others as well. You are worth loving. Your truth, however painful, can be faced.

Be intentional: reach out to family who loves you. Maybe that doesn't include all the people who share your DNA. If not, there's your first step: find a circle of women to love you and help you hold your head up. Take my story, and all the stories in this book, as encouragement. Don't let shame cut you off from the love you need to heal your heart. Embrace the ones who love you. Embrace your truth. Embrace your worth!

Walking Forward in Faith

Patrice Withers-Stephens

"For I know the plans I have for you,"
declares the Lord, "plans to prosper you and not to
harm you, plans to give you hope and a future."

—*Jeremiah 29:11*

It's terminal. Hearing that is painful, brutal, gut-wrenching. What do you mean it's terminal? I questioned God. I've been praying for a healing for my father and I thought it would come. I can't make it without him. How will I continue? I want him to get better. These are all the thoughts that rushed across my mind. Is this really happening to me? Why can't bad things happen to bad people? What did I do to deserve this? Then I realized I had to armor up. Talking about putting on the full armor of God was about to have a very new definition and meaning in my life. I was going to war, a true battle with the enemy.

I had just had a beautiful weekend. In fact, I was just about to preside over my final business meeting as president of an organization, and that was totally worth a celebration. I had declared 2016 to be the year to "Believe in Greater." God was shifting and moving me to new levels that I couldn't have anticipated. The year actually turned out to be a lot of *no*s, but I was still believing in God for a *yes*. I had just wrapped up having chicken and waffles with my girl for her late birthday brunch. We had had a great afternoon. I was feeling very good, the kind of good where I felt like I could let out a sigh of relief. It was time to get Patrice's life back, I thought. Not long after I made it home, though, I got a call from my cousin, who is as close to me as a sister. Sadly, I knew it had to be something serious because we never chat on the phone. That's when she said the words: "It's terminal."

Nobody wants to have to tell you that your dad isn't doing too good and you should probably come to see him soon. But I was glad my cousin told me, as I needed to know what was going on. I hung up the phone and literally almost collapsed. I lost my breath. What was God doing to me? This was just too hard. Does God not know I'm a Daddy's girl and I need my daddy?

I was used to the bad news calls at that point, as I had been there before. It feels like every time you think maybe you're in the clear, something else comes up. I'm totally convinced the enemy comes to rob, steal, kill, and destroy all of your faith. I'll never forget getting the dreaded call from my dad just a few short days away from Christmas in 2014 to let me know he was diagnosed with cancer. It was certainly not the call I was expecting.

We had been dealing with health issues for quite some time back then, but never anything so serious. Of course, my first thought was: is he going to die? I'm strong and knowledgeable, so you know your girl thought she could fix it. "Dr. Withers-Stephens," Web-MD-certified, had this thing under control! Right? Actually, the web totally freaked me out. I became a wreck looking at all the outcomes. It became overwhelming to the point where I literally wasn't functioning. I must have cried for days because I needed to save my dad. He was always there for me, so I needed to be there for him. I'll never forget my dad being so strong while I was still struggling through processing that it was cancer. In fact, he said he didn't want to wait for the holidays to pass, he would rather get started on treatment right away. That turned out to be encouraging, because I knew I had a fighter on my hands and we could kick cancer's butt together. I never saw my dad act defeated, so that made me feel stronger, even though I was drowning on the inside. I knew 2015 was shaping up to be a crappy year.

Of course I shared what was going on with close friends. But while I was used to being there for others, when they needed me, I was getting weaker by the moment. It's amazing how others can think that, because you're a natural leader and fixer, you must be the strong one who has it all together. But this thing was getting the best of me. I remember, when 2015 rang in, thinking: "what do I have to look forward to?" This was going to be a real faith test, the kind of test where you have to stay ready because you don't know what is about to be thrown at you. It was literally going to take a miracle and many blessings for me to stay steady in the faith I had been speaking of almost all my life.

Years later, my faith journey was moving into a completely new stratosphere. I had to face my fears. The fear of losing my dad was becoming a reality. After getting that call from my cousin, I immediately booked a flight from Dallas to Charlotte. North Carolina was home, and normally I always looked forward to going home. But this time I didn't know what I would face. I decided to drop everything and go. I remember telling my employer I didn't know when I would return. My dad was my everything and no job was going to come before him.

When I arrived home two short days after getting the news, I remember being so nervous about entering that rehabilitation center. I needed a miracle. Thankfully, when I got into the room I felt a calm come over me. He was my daddy and I would love him and accept him in any condition. I immediately went into caregiver mode. I was staring at death in the face and I thought it was over, but the prayers of the righteous do availeth much. I asked God to give me the strength to help my dad to literally get up again. He was a fighter. That radiation wouldn't win. Daily, I started to see God work. We went from him being unable to get up out of the bed to him walking again. I literally saw a miracle. God said to me: it's not over until I say it's over. And, He said, you can't be in faith and worry.

Now, faith and worrying are real. I won't even begin to pretend that I didn't have a worry in me. It's very natural to feel an abundance of emotions when you truly don't know what the outcome will be. However, our faith tells us it's not a matter of feeling—and thank God my faith isn't contingent on my feelings. I'll never forget learning a valuable lesson from Sheryl Brady, my pastor at the Potter's House of North Dallas, as she spoke on faith fluctuations during a Sunday morning service in 2013. I was literally raised in the church, so I extensively knew what faith was. I knew all I needed was that mustard seed-sized faith to make it, but I had no idea it was acceptable to fluctuate in my faith. Wow! When I learned it was natural to fluctuate in faith, it was so freeing. I was also happy to know faith doesn't always make sense, but it's more about trusting the process. God has preordered every aspect of our lives, but it's so easy to worry in uncertain times. The idea of walking forward in faith means I can't survive solely on my feelings. I'm learning I have to consciously make a choice to trust God for the journey and know that He is already there so long as I keep moving forward. As Luke 1:37

tells us, faith does not make things easy, but with God all things are possible.

But how is it possible to move forward in faith while watching the person you love so much decline? I was truly on a faith journey. What was God preparing me for? One thing is sure, God has a way of backing you into a corner where you must rely on Him alone. There's literally nothing that anyone else can do for you. Only He can save you.

My breakthrough was on the way. It felt, at least, like things were finally starting to look up. Cancer may have been in my dad but it didn't own him. After all was said and done, twenty days in rehab later, Dad was up and going again, and it was encouraging. I felt like God hadn't forgotten about me. He showed me you can't predict outcomes, so stop worrying about it. The last few days in rehab were fun, with the family singing Christmas carols and eating a Carolina style Thanksgiving dinner. I felt incredibly blessed that Dad was going home just in time for Thanksgiving. Then another bombshell dropped; I had to face yet another conversation.

This conversation was a tough one; in fact, it was the worst of them all. Not because of a new health discovery, but because Dad needed me to know he was preparing for his final resting place. I can remember everything about this conversation so well. I had been strong with everything else. I never let my dad see me cry, but this conversation zapped all the life out of me. As we sat in the living room, Dad told me that he was tired, so I told him to go and lie down and get some rest. He said, "No, I don't mean that kind of tired." He was ready to go home to his place in Heaven. I mustered up enough strength to say it was okay if he wanted to. Not that I was God, but I wanted him to feel reassured that I would release him back to God, even as much as it hurt. We both cried; it was painful. He said, "I'm so proud of you and I know you'll be okay." I really didn't want to hear that because I needed him, but he had fought and the body does become weak after so long.

How in the world could I move forward in faith after getting that news? It was really too much to digest. I now needed to prepare for a major loss. I had never lost a parent. My mind was a wreck. Part of me wanted it to be well in my soul, but the other part of me was selfish. I needed my dad. He was my backbone. He was more than my dad, he was my biggest fan. What would life be like with no more calls, no more hugs, without the unconditional love that everyone longs for, where everything you do is right in a person's eyes? Was this my thank you from God? Was I being punished?

Let me just say there's no way to be prepared for a great loss. It's a defining moment in your life where you can't survive without faith. Nearly two months after that conversation,—February 7, 2017, to be exact, around 7 a.m.—I saw my dad take his last breath as he laid in the bed at a hospice house. All I could think was: Is this real? Somebody wake me up from this nightmare. I had been praying for a healing. I'm sure you're familiar with miracle stories, like when Lazarus was raised from the dead, but my dad wasn't coming back and I had to accept it.

I finally had an "ah-ha" moment after many days of trying to analyze why my prayers weren't answered. God showed me that healing comes in various forms. I used to overwhelm myself with feelings of guilt from not doing enough even as I was feeling exhausted from doing way too much. This phenomenon shouldn't exist, but it's easy to get caught up in the faith fluctuations and be left to feel inadequate. Inadequacy is something I have had to power through with this devastating loss. Every day I feel as though I'm dealing with the aftermath of the most stressful experience of my life. But faith always rises to the top and tells me I am a conqueror through Christ Jesus. In knowing this fact, it allows me to intentionally stay in the race to keep living. God heals us in many ways; it's just that those ways might be different than what we had in mind. Sometimes complete healing comes in the form of being absent from the body and being present with the Lord. I'm just starting to appreciate God's ultimate healing, but it does suck to be left behind to bear the pain.

One day the sun will shine again. New mercies are given to me daily, and for this I will continue to be grateful for each day of life, regardless of the obstacles I have to face. Psalm 63:3–4 (AMP) tells us, "Because your lovingkindness is better than life, my lips shall praise you. So I will bless you as long as I live; I will lift up my hands in your name." The testing of my faith will produce perseverance and endurance.

I love hearing the whispers from God that confirm I am enough. Faith tells me to fully trust and surrender it all over to Him. God wants us to find contentment with Him in any state of being. I now know that, while I may not enjoy my current state, I can rest in His promises. I am a work in progress. Not a scholar, but a life learner willing to live a life for Christ. I must keep walking forward in faith. In faith I can move from point A to point B; the key is to just move!

> Not that I have already obtained it or have already been made perfect, but I actively press on so that I may take hold of that for which Christ Jesus took hold of me and made me His own . . . . forgetting what lies behind and reaching forward to what lies ahead, I press on toward the goal to win the prize of the upward call of God in Christ Jesus.
>
> *Philippians 3:12–14 (AMP)*

Saving a Little for Myself

Tiffany D. Hicks

"He that getteth wisdom loveth his own soul: he that keepeth understanding shall find good."

—*Proverbs 19:8*

I've always known that I was put here to help others. When I was young, I imagined that I'd be a nurse or a teacher, something that would satisfy my desire to help people get to a new point in their lives that was better than the preceding one. Luckily for me, I had parents who fostered that desire, especially my mother. Early on, she made it clear to me that she saw that desire to help in me. I was taught to be compassionate, responsible, and independent. I was fortified with the understanding that I could do anything I put my mind to. For me, this reinforcement translated as follows: I have the ability to do anything, so I'm going to make life great for myself and those around me. I did not know it then, but this combination of parental support and encouragement paired with my own inner desire to do well for myself and others was the beginning of the development of my own little operating principal: Live life in a manner that allows me to create, build, and grow myself and everything around me. It was that simple—until it wasn't! This desire to operate in my mission became entwined in my identity in a way that was sometimes as bad for me as it was beneficial to me.

As I became older, it was my goal to never lose sight of my fundamental belief that I should get all that I could out of life, then share that bounty with others. This manifested in many ways. The good thing was that I sought out knowledge, which sparked a strong sense of creativity. I fell in love with books, art, writing, and anything that allowed me to express my creativity. All positive things that I still love today. On the other side of that, my need to be the helper became almost an obsession. My ability to give and do for others became a fixation that could only be satisfied by doing more. With family, especially my immediate family, I was fiercely protective and had a sense of obligation to ensure that they were happy. Whatever form it took, I was willing to find a way to make it happen because I felt that it was my responsibility. In my friendships, my belief manifested itself as die-hard allegiance. There were instances where it was clear that the friendship wasn't mutually beneficial, yet I found it difficult to break away even if it was clearly necessary. To me, holding up my end of the bargain meant that I should find a way to make the friendship work, and if it was broken, I needed to foster it back to health. In my personal or love relationships, it manifested as unconditional loyalty. Period. Good times or bad, it didn't matter. I was determined to stay and pour everything that I had into that relationship, with the thought that that was the way that you help it grow. This meant that there came points in relationships where I'd pour all that I had into it, even where there was a risk that I wouldn't receive what I needed in return. My goal was to stick with it at all costs, because in the end, in order to see a seed grow, you have to stick around and tend to it, right?

As you may have picked up, I developed the mindset that when you give something your all—your time, resources, energy, and love—it can't end in anything other than success. I found out, though, that this isn't always true. I have to preface what I am about to say with this: I cannot say that the people that I was in relationships with are to blame. The way that I implemented my idea of what it means to be productive in life and relationships was flawed, in small part by what I'd learned when I was young, but mostly by my own hand. The noble concept of being selfless became costly, in that there were many instances where I gave what I thought was needed to others but failed to ensure that what I kept for myself was enough to sustain me. Years of this led to flat-out burnout. I began to feel great stress. I felt as if I was losing myself and could not get leverage on identifying who I truly was. I was lost. This led me to a place of unsettledness, loneliness, and even a sense of desolation. I came to the realization that I was the common denominator in all of these relationships. There was something in me that needed to be fine-tuned. This lent itself to much internal toil, as I was working to change parts of me that were formed when I was a child. Was it right to change what seemed like such a fundamental part of my identity?

I needed to figure out how to get to a point where I could see myself as a conduit for others to reach happiness without being the vessel that held their happiness. This meant intentionally relearning how to transmit what I have to offer to others without depleting the supply of time, mental and emotional energy, financial resources, and such that I needed for myself the way that I had in the past. It has not been an easy journey. There are times when I have failed miserably at untangling what I think others need and expect of me from what I really should be offering to them.

In order to figure out what my true, most productive role should be, I took a step back from all of those relationships to get a clear view of my purpose in life and where I should fit into the lives of others. I moved halfway across the country, prayed a lot, and spent time alone getting to know myself. I took time to just be me. Having a little more knowledge today, if I could hit a reset button I would not change who I am fundamentally. I would, however, change how I implement my purpose. There are some ground rules that I commit myself to today:

Give, but not to your demise. I've learned that it's okay to be selfishly selfless. This is my way of finding balance in caring for others and myself equally. We are of absolutely no assistance to anyone if we are worn down and broken. It's important that we learn to give in a way that doesn't lead to us losing ourselves. If we wrap our entire identity around fulfilling the needs of others, we run the risk of feeling that the sole defining factor in our success as people is our ability to do for and give to others. Sometimes, you can make a perfect investment into a person and still wonder if it was "enough." This can break you down. This leads to my next point:

Know when to say no! We have to know when enough is enough. There are times when we have to separate our *desire* to do from our *ability* to do. I still live life under the thought that I am here to help, but I also know that I don't owe everyone everything! I had to learn that it is not our job to be everything to everyone. We have to set parameters and boundaries on what we can reasonably do for others without it having a negative impact on them or us. At times, our desire to say "yes" can lead to enabling those around us in a way that causes them to miss opportunities to grow or to step closer to finding ways to be self-reliant. That goes back to the conduit-vessel concept.

Understand that sometimes failure is inevitable. I am a perfectionist, so it is always my goal to win. Despite this, I am learning to be okay with a loss when I miss the mark. I spent too much of my life feeling as if I didn't have the option to fail others or myself. This is a heavy weight to bear for even the best and most seasoned among us. I have come to the realization that outside of God, perfection does not exist and I cannot make it exist. If we focus all of our effort on being perfect in relationships, we set ourselves up for failure. When all doesn't go according to plan, it's easy to become fixated on where we went wrong—even if the failure doesn't fall squarely on our shoulders. We ask questions like: Did I fail to do enough? Did I fail to invest enough? Where did I go wrong?

In some cases, our delivery, timing, or overall effort may be off. When we know this to be true, then we should certainly course-correct to avoid that same thing in the future. More often than not, though, it's not the giver that is unsuccessful. Sometimes what we have to offer others is not what they need at the moment, sometimes they are not prepared to manage the gift, and sometimes they are just plain not worthy. The latter cases are no reflection on you, so recognize it and move forward!

Give from your cup, not your well. This sounds odd, but hear me out! Our well is our reserve. It's what we draw from to sustain ourselves in our times of need. Metaphorically, our wells house joy, peace, love, emotional wellbeing, and everything or anything else we need a supply of to make it through our day-to-day lives. Literally, we also have tangible wells that contain what we need to sustain ourselves financially, physically, and materially.

When our well has a supply, we are able to fill our cup to capacity as needed. When we are mindful of our supply, there is more than enough for us to drink from the cup and to share freely with others. This means that we can and should give from our cup freely and without hesitation. When the metaphorical or literal cup that we have becomes low or empty, it is our responsibility to ourselves to check our well to see if there is still a supply before we make another move to refill the cup. If our well's supply remains plentiful, we can refill the cup and offer to others as needed. The mistake that we often make is that we give from our cups when our well is empty because we fail to assess our well to see if there is enough left to give. Therefore, in our hopeless desire to help others, there are times when we are careless and we end up trying to refill the cup from a well that is empty.

The danger in that is not in giving—giving is a great thing. The danger lies in the fact that if we give to the point where we empty our well, we don't have a supply left for anyone, not even ourselves. An empty well is useless. In the natural sense, a well with no water isn't able to serve its primary purpose—to provide a life-sustaining substance that is essential to our survival. On the other side, emptying a well that should contain a store of our metaphorical or literal resources can be detrimental. Be sure to leave enough for yourself.

Burnout is real and manifests in many forms. We often hear quotes and analogies about never giving up, staying the course, and never getting weary. What we rarely hear is how to do that without completely burning ourselves out. I learned the hard way that burnout is real, and there are a few different types of burnout that I experienced. The first was relationship burnout. Simply put, I spent so much time and effort on trying to ensure that every relationship that I was involved in was "perfect" that I'd develop a sense of unrest at the thought of interacting with the people that I loved. Then, there was generosity burnout. Because I'd come to equate the health of my relationships with how much I gave, I got to a point where giving no longer brought me joy but instead felt like a requirement and a burden. Finally, the combination of relationship and generosity burnout led me to come to the point of personal burnout. For me, this was the worst. Because there was no "perfect," I began to feel a sense of failure each time an aspect of a relationship didn't go as I thought it should. This led me down a path of self-doubt, withdrawal, and discontentment in my life. I didn't feel the sense of fulfillment that I wanted to. This was not because of the actions of those that I was in relationships with. They, for the most part, felt fine with things as they were. The struggle was internal.

To overcome the burnout I was experiencing, it was my responsibility to create balance. We all know the saying "It's better to give than receive." I agree with this to an extent, because it goes back to what I felt in my formative years—my purpose is to help. In saying that, though, it's important to remember that there are times when we need to be on the other end of giving. Relationships are reciprocal. We all need deposits.

We are responsible for one another, I cannot stress that enough. We are, however, only able to offer care to others effectively when we understand how to care for ourselves first. A broken vessel cannot hold anything, and therefore it can't pour out. We each bring gifts to the table that are designed to help us fulfill our purpose on this Earth. If we don't care for ourselves first, we aren't able to properly implement those gifts, which means that the world cannot benefit from all that we have to offer.

Never Give Up

Brigid Roberson

"Nothing in this world is worth having or worth doing unless it means effort, pain, difficulty."

—*Theodore Roosevelt*

As a young girl I grew up in a very small town with a population of two thousand people. It was the country, as we considered it, and everyone looked out for each other without regard to relation or color of skin. My family didn't have much, no designer clothes, shoes, or handbags, but my dad kept a clean Chevrolet Monte Carlo that shone like it was brand new. When we moved from a single-story trailer to a double wide, I thought we were big stuff, when in fact we were just ordinary, or, in today's terms, we were low income.

I learned at a very early age to appreciate everything, work hard, make good grades, and be thankful for all my blessings. My parents instilled in me to put God first, help others, do the best you can, and, most importantly, never give up. We were disciplined kids who had to be in the house at exactly the curfew hour, not a minute late. We had to earn things that our children take for granted in today's society. This built character and the basic infrastructure for my work ethic and moral aptitude to always be kind and help others. I was constantly involved in many activities at the school; my goal was to eventually move away from our small town to try to make something of myself, and not have another generation of having babies without a means to provide for them except welfare or being unemployed.

My grandmother, mother, and aunts were all housekeepers for some of the rich families in the area and had worked for years doing so, because in that small town there were not very many jobs available. For all the work done, they did not receive much pay. I knew from a young age that that profession was not going to work for me. My strict father worked in the oil field and had also served in the US Army in Vietnam. As a family of six struggling to make ends meet, we were gracious recipients of the welfare system and food stamps. We couldn't wait until the first of the month when we could get fresh groceries and some of our favorite things. Yet our love for each other and family was worth more than money could buy.

No one in our family had graduated from college before I went; although some had attended, none had graduated. Really, college wasn't talked about much nor explored in depth, especially not historically black colleges. My friends that knew and understood the importance of college were predominantly white and Hispanic. I remember being told to consider the top predominantly white institutions (PWIs), not a historically black college, in order to get better jobs upon college graduation. I was in the top ten percent of my class, so I could attend the college of my choice. After my research in 1983, I chose Texas State University, a PWI, for that reason.

When I got to college, I cried my eyes out when my parents drove off and left me at my school because it was my first time away from them. All of a sudden my country ass didn't know if I really wanted to go to college there or not. I was afraid of the next chapter of my life. I knew I couldn't give up, though, because I would have to go home. I feared being a domestic with little pay.

My friendliness took me a long way. I met my college suitemate, who was a very refined and beautiful black girl who had graduated from a Catholic high school for girls and was an aspiring attorney. I remember telling her that I was going to study physical therapy, but later I decided that learning about all those bones and joints was not for me. I felt inadequate compared to her and some of the other black girls who were in my dorm, because it seemed as though they were well off, that they had attended much better schools and had many more opportunities, resources, and experiences than I had had. But I would continue to hold my head up, as my mom would say, and use my country etiquette and friendly smile to make friends with them. I made it into the school on an academic and track scholarship. Initially, I was apprehensive with girls who were faster than me on the track team, and the class sizes were very large compared to the eighteen to twenty people that were in the classrooms at home.

It was in college that I started to learn more about my culture. I joined a predominantly African American sorority, which helped to mold me into a greater person, and resolved that service to all mankind is one of the best hallmarks of life.

I went on to learn more about my culture, and of the wrong sort—and began doing more partying and less studying. As a result, my grades plummeted, and I did not want to run track any more. I told my mother that I was going to quit, and she said, "you started it, so you finish it." Regrettably, I did quit for that year. I had to work to pay for school after losing that scholarship, so I started working part time at one job and full time at another, leaving very little time to study for classes or participate in my extracurricular activities.

I had finally landed on my major being communications because it came very naturally to me. I was always involved with community service and helping others at both the job corps and around the city. I went on to graduate, and became the first in my family to do so. My family was so proud; my whole family came to show their pride and support. I immediately got a job, but was highly disappointed that it was not the high-paying job that I had envisioned based on what I had been told. It was only entry-level pay. This was devastating, considering I had loans to pay back.

A few months after starting work, I received a call from my mom. The unthinkable had happened; my dad was killed while working on the job. I went home to be there for my mom. All of sudden, I had to be the responsible one, handling all the business, and making sure my mom was taken care of. It was hard. I will never forget the day it really sank in; the sheriff came over to deliver my dad's clothes and there was still blood on them. He would never get to walk me down the aisle or see my son be born.

My focus became being the leader of the family instead of living a young and carefree life. My mom depended on me now to handle her business and financial affairs. This meant I had to mature quickly. I was scared, and I didn't want to fail my mom, my number one fan. I remember reading Joshua 1:9 and being inspired by it: "Have I not commanded you? Be strong and courageous. Do not be afraid; do not be discouraged, for the Lord your God will be with you wherever you go." I knew God was with me; there were times that I wasn't in the right place, dated the wrong guys, or made bad decisions as people in their twenties do, but every time God had mercy on me.

I started making better decisions. I began working as a caseworker for a program that would allow me to help women go from welfare to self-sufficiency. I could relate to them because I had seen it all my life with my own family. I just wanted them to know that they could do so much better if they tried. My grandmother used to say "nothing beats a failure but a try." I would use this quote for the women I worked with while showing them how to get on their feet and be independent. I would share my own personal stories to motivate them to higher levels. It was so rewarding, seeing their transition and the impact of my work. However, I wasn't advancing in my career, nor was I making the money that I desired. So I ventured out and started my own business with my mom.

Things were rolling for me after that, as I was fortunate enough to meet the love of my life and we married after three years of dating. It didn't take long before our bundle of joy arrived. Shortly after my son was able to walk and talk, I transitioned back into the workforce. My desire was still to make an impact with girls and women, and I was achieving that through community service, but still not quite on the level I wanted. I started working my way up the corporate ladder in a male-dominated field and making good money. Unfortunately, I was passed over at least three times for some executive-level jobs by men who had military or police experience. I would ask myself, why am I not good enough? So I fought back and went back to school for my master's. This degree helped me to finally conquer an executive-level job in security. The problem, though, was that I wasn't fulfilled on the inside. I had a burning desire to learn more, to advance even further in my career, but I would need training or to go back to school again.

I didn't want to pursue school at the time because I wanted to seek advancement in my community service organization. So I went for it. I tried, and I lost. The loss showed me that it was not my time. I never felt so inadequate in all my life. I cried for days and felt like I had failed not only me, but also so many others who believed in me. It showed me that God has the plan for my life; I am not the author, He is. I just needed to stop trying to be the boss of God.

It was devastating, and a hurt that I had not experienced since the loss of my dad. I really couldn't explain it to anyone because I felt that I had failed. To encourage me, my girlfriend sent me a video called "Finding Your Purpose in Life and Living Your Dream," by Oprah Winfrey. I was deeply inspired by it to keep pressing on, because God makes no mistakes and has ordered my steps. I had promised God that if I didn't move up, I would focus on becoming better and stronger by going back to school for my doctorate. I was hopeful this terminal degree would teach me how to be a better leader. I also made a promise to myself that I would work on fulfilling my greatest passion, to start a foundation for girls, and concentrating on being a better me. I was intentional in my thoughts, in my mind, and in my actions.

I got accepted into a prestigious doctoral program at a very low point in my life and I knew it was God picking me up once again. I didn't deserve it, but He saved me anyway. I had given so much of myself to friends, family, and so many other things that I had forgotten about self-preservation. I had forgotten about taking care of myself physically and emotionally. I had lost excessive weight, had hypertension, and was emotionally drained because I was moving too fast. To pick myself up, I would lean heavily on God's voice in silence, song, scripture, and my Sunday morning Facebook posts. My Facebook became my blog to encourage others who may have needed uplifting just as I did. It also allowed me to be encouraged by others. We were blessing each other.

I surrendered to my faith, my passion, and God's will. I was intentional and started Bridge2Greatness, Incorporated, a 501(c)(3) nonprofit designed to provide resources and mentoring opportunities for at-risk girls to help them succeed. I knew that I could make a positive difference in their lives with my program. I just needed to muster up enough energy and support to take on this critical project and yield the desired impact. There were some challenges, but we stayed the course to success, knowing that giving up was not an option. After researching the school-to-prison pipeline for African American girls at schools, I was even more inspired and determined to take on this major task. The board of directors and I began planning a four-day conference that would build the girls up, provide workshops with guest speakers, and include a hotel stay with food free of charge. A major component of the program was the teen summit, which featured a panel of professionals who discussed and answered questions from our teen participants about their specific careers. The summit was a huge success because it also involved other teens of many different ages, including college students who held a forum on teen issues such as sexting, bullying, self-confidence, and dating. Our program had a special component where we taught the girls how to give back to the community by building bears with special get-well messages for children in the hospital who had cancer. We were featured three times on the local news station and the girls were so thrilled. Our culminating event included the girls gaining a mentor who would support them after the conference, receiving a special set of pearls presented by their mentors which signified their own inner beauty and strength, and having a fashion show that highlighted just how beautiful each of them are. The girls and their parents were truly grateful for the opportunity. Little did they know, I was just as grateful to the girls for building me up and blessing me. I had finally fulfilled my purpose and passion in life. I was overjoyed with the success and how much I had overcome to fulfill my destiny.

Oprah Winfrey stated, "You have to know what sparks the light in you so that you, in your own way, can illuminate the world." Helping others is what truly drives my success. It gives me the fuel to keep going when I have run out of energy. My work to provide positive people and influences in the lives of young girls will reap life-long impacts.

My life has taken on many different twists, turns, ups, downs, highs, and lows. My personal goals have also taken a circuitous route, overcoming obstacles, defeat, and other setbacks before landing on my passion, Bridge2Greatness. Through all the highs and lows in life, it is the lows that tested me beyond what I had been taught. I was pretty close to abandoning the way entirely, basically having a pity party all by myself in my mind. I went into deep reflection, and remembered a quote attributed to St. Ignatius Loyola, "go forth and set the world on fire." I never gave up or gave in, although there were many times that I felt like I was pretty close. The one constant that never changed was God's promise to never leave me—and I don't believe He brought me this far to leave me.

Be Open to Change

LaTisha Terry

"I can do all things through Christ who strengthens me."

—*Philippians 4:13 (NKJV)*

For the last ten years, I have worked in the financial industry in a leadership position. Working with customers on a daily basis, I began to notice a common theme among them: most of them were clueless about how to manage their finances, or they were in a financial bind they didn't know how to get out of. I found myself going above and beyond to help customers in any way I possibly could. It took me awhile to acknowledge that this was my calling. With everything I learned while working in the industry and my previous interests, I decided to launch my own company, Fancy Chat.

At a young age, I had dreams of becoming an acclaimed news anchor for CNN. When I went to college, it was only right that I majored in communications. In 2006, when I graduated from Alabama A&M University with a bachelor's degree, I was a very naive and eager twenty-something-year-old ready to conquer the world. With no job or a real plan for how I would make this happen, I moved back home to Milwaukee, Wisconsin. Coming home afforded me the opportunity to obtain three internships that would help me get on the path to becoming a news anchor. I interned at the news station and the radio station, and I was an on-air personality for a show on ESPNU. I knew for sure that gaining this experience would help me with my dream of becoming a news anchor. I made numerous resume tapes and sent them all over the country but did not receive any callbacks. That prideful twenty-something girl was slowly beginning to lose her confidence. Fortunately, I was able to land a job as a floor assistant at the same news station where I interned. Jackpot! This position allowed me to build relationships with people who could assist me with creating a great resume tape! Such were my thoughts. So, on my days off, I would partner with reporters and work on new material to send to producers.

Once my resume tape was complete, I reached out to someone I considered a mentor to ask if she could watch my tape and give me some feedback—constructive feedback. After reviewing my tape, she said, "Honey, I would only hire you because you're pretty, not because you have any real talent." I was crushed to say the least. For a moment, she had me thinking that my life goal was unattainable because I didn't have talent. This broken girl went home and shed more tears. Thank God for my mother, who has always encouraged me and built me up when the world tried to tear me down. Because of her encouragement and her belief in me, I felt confident enough to give my tape to someone else for review, and in return, this individual provided some very useful feedback.

Now, I wasn't the rock star that I thought I was, but I had the skills, knowledge, and power to become one. So, I sent more tapes—and still crickets. By that time, I was fed up and way past emotional. I couldn't understand why I wasn't getting any callbacks. However, it gave me time to take a closer look at my dream job. Was this really something that I still wanted to do? I would see the type of women that were on TV and they really didn't look like me. I wasn't ready to transform who I was just to be on television. It also became apparent to me how impersonal the news made me feel. I couldn't see myself knocking on the door of family members who just lost a loved one just to get a story. That's when I realized that Tisha needed a plan B. It never occurred to me to have a backup plan because I was certain that my original plan was what was best, and there was nothing that could deter me from that. Now it was time to take a step back and figure out what else I could do. What was I really good at? Finally, I made the decision to attend graduate school, and I enrolled in the MBA program at Cardinal Stritch University. At that point, I still had no clue what I wanted to achieve in life, but the program would offer me a variety of opportunities. Overall, the whole process was a challenge, but it allowed me to tap into some of my other talents as well as boost my confidence in certain areas, such as financing.

While in grad school, I experienced a devastating loss when someone very close to me was murdered. That was the first time I completely detached from everything. I could only ask, why me? Why is it ALWAYS ME?! This situation played a vital role in my life. Everyone experiences and deals with pain and loss in a different way. And it's always hard to fully articulate how you feel. For years, I experienced a high level of confusion. Eventually, like with many other painful things that I've dealt with, I just learned to live with it. This is not always the best thing to do. Too often we are taught to keep things to ourselves to avoid being a burden to others. We have to realize that it's okay to reach out for help when it's needed. It doesn't make you weak to ask for help. I kept all of my feelings bottled up inside and never shared how I was truly feeling. That in turn set me back emotionally; I was scared to start dating again for fear I would lose another person I loved. It also pulled on emotions of losing my father at a young age. I can only wish I had spoken to someone who specialized in the grieving process; they could have helped me more smoothly deal with my loss.

During my last year of school, I started a career in banking. I was beyond excited to start a career, and to move forward from just having a job. Ironically enough, while it wasn't my original dream, I could always see myself being a bank teller. My sister worked in the financial industry when

I was younger, and I thought it was the coolest job on earth. I finished grad school with an MBA and a brand-new plan!

Early on in my banking career I had good mentors, and I quickly moved up to management. Although management was pretty challenging at times, it was also very rewarding. I fell in love with the ability to coach people and help them achieve their personal career goals. I was slowly but surely starting to realize what I actually enjoyed in life—helping people. During this time, I was transitioning into becoming more involved in church. Not as much as I should have or was called to, but I was making baby steps. I became more involved with community events and engaged in networking. I enjoyed my career and the path it was taking, but it was time for me to grow.

Relocating had always been an option for me, but it had to make sense. This would be a huge decision that would take me away from my family, my comfort zone. I knew that if I was going to step out on faith and make the decision to relocate, I had to be open to change. God gives us so many opportunities to exercise our faith, but we miss them and then wonder why we have so many unexplained issues. We have to focus on faith, and not our own understanding of things. I finally exhausted all options, prayed daily, and decided it was time to go, but where? Research, research, research. I looked into areas that were up and coming for business professionals and places where the cost of living was reasonable. I landed on some great places, and ultimately, I chose Dallas, Texas! I can't thank God enough for allowing me so many opportunities to get out of my own way, landing me here in Texas.

I often tell people the journey getting here wasn't easy. I literally packed up all I could fit in my 2008 Toyota Corolla and drove seventeen hours to get to Dallas. It took me about a year to finally get comfortable in my living conditions, and I still miss my family like crazy, but God has rewarded me repeatedly for my faithfulness. Since moving to Dallas, I have had the opportunity to involve myself in a lot of networking, which has resulted in meeting some good people. I continued my career in retail banking, but was looking for an opportunity to do something different. I have always had big dreams for myself, and retiring as a branch manager was not one of them. So what could I do? I still had a strong passion for broadcast journalism, but I've always enjoyed the satisfaction of helping someone with his or her financial needs. This time, when considering my next career move, I took the time to really pray and meditate before I made a decision.

When you begin to pray and separate yourself from your surroundings, you can hear God speak to you. You are able to see the things He has available for you, just by being aware.

Over the past ten years, I was so distracted because things were not going according to MY plan. I had no idea that it was part of God's plan all along. Throughout the process, I was gaining tangible skills that would help me to live out my purpose. I realized that my ministry is the ministry of giving, and that is what Fancy Chat represents. When you think of financial literacy, it entails so much, and many people have no idea where to begin. Fancy Chat was built to provide people with the knowledge to become financially sound. What originally started as a blog is now definitely more than just that, it's a brand. Fancy Chat is here to provide knowledge, and empower you to be the very best you! This brand is my personal testimony of the good, the bad, and the ugly, as well as things I enjoy doing. What we see on television and social media is everyone at their best, and people feel pressure to match that. I would love us to get back to the basics and set goals in life to encourage people to be whatever they want to be, to teach people about finances and their options. If someone has made bad financial decisions in the past, it does not mean that they cannot move forward and obtain the things they desire. In an effort to reach an audience that would prefer to gain knowledge by listening as opposed to reading, Fancy Chat has started a podcast. The podcast includes interviews with people that are experienced in different areas, such as taxes, financial aid, marketing and public relations, and much more.

My whole life has been about being open to change and not being afraid to step out on faith. At times life gets hard, and it looks like things or situations won't change. Understand, we all go through seasons, and some are worse than others; but like any storm, they don't last forever, and the aftermath is beautiful. As Dr. Jatun states in her book, *Intentional Living: 30 Productivity Principles to Achieve Peace of Mind*, "Sometimes, it is imperative to change the way we think, see, and do things." Had I not been open to the many changes that have taken place in my life, I would not be where I am today.

Navigating the Corporate Majority as a Minority

Floyd Dorsey IV

"Success is to be measured not so much by the position that one has reached in life as by the obstacles which he has overcome while trying to succeed."

—*Booker T. Washington*

When the perpetual cycle of systematic life promotion ends, that is where life begins. Matriculating through the school system—elementary, middle school, high school, undergraduate, and even postgraduate school—is a pre-paved road map that sets minimum requirements to complete to receive a reward. The majority of society, those that have gone through the process and attained high scholastic achievement and those that may have fallen short of their goals, underpins the system. Within the educational system, there are requirements for various disciplines, which are demonstrated by the mandatory courses one must complete and the minimal grade that should be achieved. The rewards are promotions to the next grade level through graduation and the new body of knowledge garnered through the process. As people venture through the system, they obtain a mindset of promotional gratification and thus may be unprepared for the shock that awaits them in the real world.

As I went through the perpetual cycle, my parents constantly enforced academic and athletic excellence. Taking heed of their guidance, I often received accolades for my achievements within the classroom and on the football field. One of my crowning accomplishments was being offered a full scholarship from multiple Division I collegiate institutions. After finishing high school, I elected to attend Tulane University, where I played football and started all four years as a defensive end. Maintaining the tenet of excellence enforced by my parents, I continued to receive accolades for accomplishments both on and off the football field. At this point, my expectations for life were deeply rooted in what the educational system had taught me: simply follow the pre-paved roadmap, exceed the minimum requirements, and you'll be promoted to the next level. Who was I to question the process? It was even reinforced by the ones that loved me most. Upon graduation, life took an interesting turn. I began to ask some of the most basic yet fundamental questions, like who am I, and where am

I going? While meeting with a close friend, during one of our frequent weekly meet-ups, I asked a question that took me several years to answer. The question was simply: how do you be? We were both perplexed, as we began to articulate what we thought were suitable answers, but nothing we came up with would quench our thirst at the time.

I was a recent college graduate in search of employment and, more importantly, no longer in the cycle of systematic life promotion. While in the school system I knew how to be, and I was yearly rewarded and promoted to the next rung for my efforts. What I didn't know was how to be a successful black man when navigating the corporate structure, looking to achieve similar success to what I had in the prior phases of my life. As I began to explore career opportunities, I reflected on a part of my past experiences in academia and athletics that was not a concern then, but became one in my corporate experience. In academia, my grades spoke for themselves; in football, my performance evidenced my skill. However, in the corporate world, despite performance ratings and skills, there was the perceived challenge of being a black male. While there were many males in senior-level positions, not many looked like me. I was looking for a roadmap or a system that would allow me to continue to be oblivious to the stark reality that I was eventually forced to face. I spent a little over a year in New Orleans, Louisiana, after graduating; during that time, I worked five part-time jobs until I accepted a full-time job offer in Texas. I was excited about relocating back to Texas and, most importantly, starting a new career in the financial services industry. The job was entry level but came with high demands. My contentment with the role lasted about four months, until I really started to evaluate my surroundings and professional goals.

There were many recent college graduates working alongside of me, the majority being African American; however, as mentioned earlier, the demographics drastically changed up the leadership chain. Observing this created great doubt for my intentions to climb the corporate ladder and eventually obtain a senior leader role. There was a random encounter with one of the supervisors, who was also a black male, which reinforced my doubts. He asked me what my plans were while with the organization, and my reply was to become a senior leader. He chuckled with a hint of sarcasm, which led me to believe that it wouldn't happen. That was a pivotal moment in my early career that awakened me to the fact that, if I continued to perform as I had been, there was no way I would climb the corporate ladder. I was forced to take a step back and have an objective moment of self-reflection.

I decided that it was time for a change, and then revisited the question "how do you be" and began searching inside and outside the organization to find senior leaders, regardless of gender or race, who were in roles that I aspired to one day attain. While I was not clear on my future profession or dream job, I was clear that I wanted to lead people and solve problems, and that I enjoyed the financial services industry. The leaders that I examined were excelling in my areas of interest. I wanted to know how they think and what they do. If I aspired to be in a comparable position to them, my thoughts and actions had to be similar. I requested informational sessions with the leaders to engage with them, glean best practices, and build relationships. I was eager to learn and was like a sponge, absorbing every ounce of wisdom shared during the sessions. It was during that dialogue and overtime that I began to notice how the leaders' level of thinking was more comprehensive, how relationships and reputation are key, and how important it is to learn as much as possible in every role that I have during my career. Those sessions proved to me that common characteristics of leaders were consistent regardless of race; however, as I had identified earlier on, there was also a clear indication of limited opportunity for black men to achieve senior level.

I learned what leaders do, and that how they spent their time was different than junior-level employees. They developed and nurtured meaningful relationships with other like-minded individuals and spent a considerable amount time focused on improving their business acumen. After enlightening dialogue, I was inspired to expand my way of thinking and overall wellbeing as a professional. This is where the "doing" came into play, again. I purchased several books, including *7 Habits of Highly Effective People* by Stephen Covey and *4-Hour Work Week* by Timothy Ferris, which provided more insight into the path I desired to travel and the anticipated transition.

I developed both short- and long-term goals and identified resources that would enable my trajectory in achieving them. They were written down and easily accessible to stand as a constant reminder of my ultimate goal. Once my goals were clear, I employed the following key steps that enhanced my thinking and doing and led to a new state of being in a professional realm.

THINKING:

1. **Continuous self-improvement.** It became clear that my individual professional development required helping others achieve their goals and assisting the company with advancement, as well as preparing myself to move up the ladder. Regardless of whether things were going well or not, I challenged myself to find opportunities for improvement. I reflected on years as a competitive athlete and was reminded that there is always room for improvement, but also, most importantly, that I should proactively seek those lessons, fix the problems, and teach others what I've learned. Remembering the core principles of being on a team, I would often think of ways to help other people and the company become more successful.

2. **Foresight and vision.** Growing up with humble beginnings, my vision was constantly challenged because of the impoverished environment; it

seemed like there were limited options. Therefore, at times I felt my sight impaired my vision or that my imagination was limited by the physical reality I faced. Prior to making the transition, I was solely focused on present situations and my thinking would typically drift in various directions. Understanding the need for foresight and vision, I learned to block out many of the distracting thoughts and look beyond the immediate circumstances to project and focus on an image of my future desired state.

3. **Strategic thinking.** I realized that my thinking was limited to tactical approaches and was not comprehensive in nature. To overcome this, I spent more time thinking through my career plans, outlining the steps required, and even consulting with trusted advisors for feedback. Each goal consisted of three options outlining a path to my goals, in addition to potential roadblocks and how I would circumnavigate the hurdles. By thinking more strategically, I began to see both the forest and the trees, understand the cause and effect of my plans, and employ deductive reasoning when addressing complex challenges.

DOING:

1. **Associations.** I reevaluated the people that I spent the majority of my time with both inside and outside of the workplace. Although I never turned my back on a friend, it was imperative that I turned more toward individuals who were on a similar path (peers and support), had achieved what I was seeking to accomplish (mentors and sponsors), or were in the earlier stages of their development and seeking to grow (mentees). It was and still is imperative that I nurture these relationships, as they are key to achieving any level of success.

2. **Education and Training.** I decided to continue my education and pursue an MBA, meanwhile proactively seeking opportunities to take on more responsibilities at work. One of my short-term goals was to become a supervisor. As a result, I began asking my manager to allow me to perform some of her duties, which incrementally increased over time. I figured that I would learn my next role while excelling in my current role.

3. **Presentation.** When I examined how the senior leaders presented themselves, I realized that I was missing the mark. There were two things that I had to address: my physical presentation and my ability to verbally communicate succinctly and effectively.

Though the saying is cliché, I truly began to dress for the position I wanted. I would also practice presenting information and request feedback from others on my verbal communication. After incorporating the feedback, I would continue the process of improvement, because I realized the power of effective communication. When someone lends you their attention, you have a small window of opportunity; therefore, choose your words wisely and make an impact.

Because of employing these key steps, I enhanced my Thinking, which influenced my Doing and ultimately changed my Being. The overall experience played a significant role in developing my personal mantra: Think, Do, Be, Do, Have™. While maintaining my core principles and integrity, I became someone completely different than I was when I first started my career. My trajectory changed, and as a result, I was promoted six times over the following three years, my annual salary quadrupled, and I obtained an MBA. My most valued accomplishment was realizing that, although I was no longer in the perpetual cycle of systematic life promotion, I was equipped with the tools and skills to chart my own path. I became more deliberate and intentional in my thoughts and actions. Through consistent application of the previously referenced steps, better thinking led to better doing, which developed a better version of me. As I became better, my actions became even more deliberate, which enables me to have a more fulfilling career.

Education Matters

Dr. Tara Peters

> "Education is the most powerful weapon, which you can use to change the world."
>
> —*Nelson Mandela*

At sixteen, I was a teenage mom. At thirty-six, I was a PhD. How does that happen? The power of education was a key component. Because of values instilled by my parents, I knew that education was my golden ticket. Not only could no one take my education away from me, but it would also allow me to chart a course for myself and my son that would allow us to attain our dreams and realize our God-given potential. Were there tough days? Were there sleepless nights? Were there times when I wasn't sure I would make it? Of course! But with the support and love of family, a relentless personal focus on achieving my dreams, and God's favor, I made it!

Today, I'm an incredibly proud mom. My son has graduated from the University of Miami and Howard University School of Law. Generra is now an attorney and aspiring entrepreneur. As I reflect on my journey from teen mom to PhD, I have gleaned insights and lessons that I hope are helpful to you. So, I'm going to share my views on why education matters from three perspectives: The Big Ones, The Global Context, and The Way Forward.

THE BIG ONES

There are several definitions for life-defining moments, but I call them "The Big Ones," those major events in your life that have shaped your path and who you are. Here's a story about one of my "Big Ones:"

I grew up in a loving family, and while my parents divorced when I was three, I always knew that my mom and dad loved me and that I was talented. As a child, my parents always stressed the importance of education; I loved school and had always done well. So, when I learned that I was pregnant, I continued to take my Advanced Placement (AP) courses and to attend classes at South Grand Prairie High School in Texas. Counselors suggested that I take classes at the high school for pregnant girls, but my family and I said no. I couldn't take my AP classes if I enrolled at that high school, and while I was going to be a teen mom, we knew that didn't affect my brain. So, I went to school with my big belly, wiggled into the desks, and focused on my studies.

While I was disappointed in myself for getting pregnant and disappointing my parents and family, I wasn't defeated. I still believed in myself and knew that I wanted to beat the odds.

The statistics for teen pregnancy are disheartening. In 2012, the National Campaign to Prevent Teen and Unplanned Pregnancies reported the following from a compilation of research studies:

- Only thirty-eight percent of teen girls who have a child before age eighteen get a high school diploma by age twenty-two.

- Less than two percent of young teen mothers attain a college degree by age thirty.

- Children born to mothers younger than eighteen years old score significantly worse on measures of school readiness, including math and reading tests.

I knew that I didn't want to be a statistic. This was a major source of motivation to further my education and to attain my PhD. It was not easy. I worked full-time while earning my doctoral degree and raising my son as a single parent. Because I had decided to pursue a career in higher education, I knew that, as an African American female, I would need the PhD credential in order to have access and opportunity. So, in retrospect, my decision to continue taking my AP classes was one of "The Big Ones" in my life because it focused my attention on the importance of challenging myself academically.

SELF-REFLECTION EXERCISE

Let's take a moment to think and reflect. There's lots of research on the power of self-reflection and carving out time to think. So, grab a journal or something to record your thoughts and then respond to the following questions:

1. What are your life-defining moments, "The Big Ones?"

2. How have they affected your life in the past and present?

3. How do you want them to affect you in the future?

Think about your response to the final question and the actionable steps you can take. Then, be intentional. Make a plan and have an accountability partner. Both will help to ensure inertia doesn't set in and will increase the likelihood you'll actually act.

THE GLOBAL CONTEXT

"Education is the new global currency" is a phrase that's being kicked around; it reflects the fact that education has value and significance worldwide. This recognition of the importance of education in a global context is seen both in grades K-12 and in higher education. The National Education Association has published an educator's guide entitled "Preparing 21st Century Students for a Global Society" and the Lumina Foundation has established Goal 2025, where "60% of Americans will hold high-quality degrees, certificates, or other postsecondary credentials by 2025" (Merisotis 2013, para. 6).

Teaching internationally has reinforced the importance of education in a global context. Northwood University, where I teach, has international program centers in several countries, and I've had the wonderful opportunity to teach undergraduate and graduate students in our programs in Montreux, Switzerland. I first began teaching internationally in 2005. Dr. Lance Watson, Dean of International Programs at the time, was visiting our campus in Texas during the fall semester. During a meeting, I casually mentioned to Dr. Watson that I was interested in teaching internationally. He talked with me about the program in Montreux, Switzerland, and then asked me to send him an email expressing my interest. Honestly, I wasn't sure if anything would happen, but I gave it a shot and sent the email. A few weeks later, I received an offer to teach a management class in December. I was elated! I was a little nervous about traveling alone, but I talked to a colleague who'd made the trip solo several times; at the end of our discussions, I was more comfortable and ready to go for it.

This experience has influenced my life in a couple of important ways. First, I have a greater appreciation for those who speak multiple languages. English is my only language, and in some respects I've been spoiled as an American because English is so widely spoken internationally. Being in class with students where English was their third or fourth language has taught me to appreciate not only the beauty of language, but also the commitment and skill that's required to master a new language, orally and in writing. This experience has made me a better educator. I'm more empathetic, I listen more intently, and my view of the world has been broadened.

Additionally, traveling solo pushed me out of my comfort zone. I've always loved to travel and had an opportunity to travel extensively growing up; however, I was usually with my family, friends, or a church group. So, I was uncomfortable with the idea of traveling alone and navigating all of the transit logistics. However, my experience traveling to teach internationally was liberating. I successfully navigated all of the logistics of the trip alone, from making my connection in Amsterdam to the ninety-minute train ride from Geneva to Montreux. At the time, I didn't recognize it as a significant moment in my life, but it was consequential. Not only did I have the opportunity to teach students from various countries in Europe and Asia and to gain a greater appreciation of international culture and history, but I also began to see myself as an international faculty member and grew in terms of my willingness to try something new by traveling solo.

While I've talked about why education in a formal context matters, I want to emphasize that it matters informally as well. Let me explain. Not all education takes place in the classroom. We have opportunities every day to be educated and to learn. One of the most important non-classroom lessons I learned was on a train ride from Casablanca Airport in Morocco to my hotel. This was my first trip to northern Africa, and I had just finished my amazing visit to the pyramids in Giza. As I was boarding the train, I noticed the heat was stifling; it felt like Texas in the heart of summer. I began to sweat and took out some tissues to wipe my forehead. As I settled into my seat, I noticed a woman dressed in traditional Muslim attire. She was wearing a black hijab and a veil covered her face. Her husband and son accompanied her on the train. She sat on the empty seat in front of me while her husband and son sat across the aisle. As she sat down, I noticed that she began to shake her veil; it appeared to me that she was fanning to cool herself in the heat. I offered her a tissue and she thanked me. She then asked me, "Are you Filipino?" I responded that I was an American. She then said, "I've never met an American."

I don't remember how I responded, but I recall being stunned that she had not met an American before. In my American-centric view of the world, I had mistakenly assumed that everyone had met an American; it never occurred to me that that might not be true. This moment was eye-opening for me because it caused me to begin to rethink some of my assumptions and views about the world. In my ignorance, I had made an erroneous assumption. Moreover, what if I had been rude or indifferent, or assumed that as a Muslim, the woman and her family were somehow dangerous? I often share this story with my graduate students during class because I want to encourage them to look for daily opportunities to be enlightened and to question deeply held assumptions.

My global experiences, both inside and outside the classroom, have been instructive and life changing. This has allowed me to be more open-minded and to recognize that while others don't necessarily share my views or experiences, these differences are not a deficit. Being more open is a conscious choice that you and I make. While I'm not suggesting that you be open to everything, it's my recommendation that you intentionally identify one or more areas where there's a principal opportunity for you to be open and stretch yourself. Then, act on that chance to grow.

SELF-REFLECTION EXERCISE

Let's take another occasion for self-reflection with a self-assessment. Openness to experience is one of the Big Five personality traits and it has been widely researched. According to psychologist Art Markman as quoted in an article by Drake Baer (2013), openness to experience is a measure of "the degree to which a person is willing to consider new ideas and opportunities." The article goes on to discuss how openness to experience is connected to creativity. Creativity is essential to our ability to imagine, think in non-linear patterns, and solve problems in an increasingly diverse and global economy.

Go to www.truity.com/test/how-open-are-you and complete the assessment. After reviewing your results, think about how you might create opportunities to strengthen your openness to experience. For example, what can you do to become more creative or willing to try something new? What can you do to incorporate more creativity into your daily activities?

Record your responses in your journal and then select one activity you want to complete in the next thirty days. Creating this small win will give you energy and confidence to try the next thing on your list.

For more information on creativity, check out the following resources:

- Newsweek article by Po Bronson and Ashley Merryman on the Creativity Crisis.
  http://www.newsweek.com/creativity-crisis-74665

- Ted Talk on the Marshmallow Challenge
  https://www.ted.com/talks/tom_wujec_build_a_tower?language=en

THE WAY FORWARD

Adaptations of Loren Eiseley's essay, "Star Thrower" (1978), shares the story of a young man who makes a difference for the starfish that he rescues from a beach laden with starfish that have washed ashore. What's the lesson? It's clear for me as an educator. Look for daily opportunities to reach down and pick up others. In doing so, you have the opportunity not only to be helpful, but to positively affect the lives of those who may cross your path, one person at a time. My journey from teen mom to PhD has taught me that each of us has the ability to make a difference, not only in our own lives, but in the lives of others, for both present and future generations. As we look toward the future, we can certainly make a difference at the individual level, as noted in the parable. What does that look like? Well, here are my recommendations.

- Invest in Yourself and Invest in Others: As a teen mom, I made a personal investment in myself by earning a full academic scholarship to attend Texas Wesleyan University for undergraduate studies, and my loving grandmother made an investment in me by agreeing to keep my son during the week while I lived on campus and attended classes.

- Eat Your Frog and Set SMART Goals: "Eat your frog" is based on a central idea presented by Brian Tracy in his book *Eat That Frog!* The frog is the most arduous task that we need to undertake. So, stop procrastinating. Start tackling projects on your to-do list with an initial focus on the most difficult. Set SMART (Specific, Measurable, Attainable, Results-oriented, and Time-based) Goals to ensure you've created actionable objectives and you're meeting your timelines and targets. Your self-reflection exercises could be the starting point.

👉 Create Whitespace: Our lives are so busy and we're often bombarded with information and overwhelmed with tasks. So, it's essential that you create time and space to think and reflect. Be intentional and set aside an hour a day. Use this time to reflect and to be creative. "WhiteSpace is like a glass of water. Every once in a while just take a little sip" (WhiteSpaceAtWork 2018).

These recommendations are a starting place, not an exhaustive list. You may even think of other courses of action. The point is to act with intention and focus, so that you're a difference maker.

The evidence is conclusive: education matters. That has been confirmed, both in my life's journey from teen mom to PhD and by empirical research. The power of education is encapsulated in the following quote from Dr. Johnnetta B. Cole, former president of Spelman College and Bennett College:

> An education that teaches you to understand something about the world has done only half of the assignment. The other half is to teach you to do something about making the world a better place.

Awakening Purpose

T'Edra Z. Jackson

"In the final analysis, it is between you and God. It was never between you and them anyway."

—*Mother Teresa*

My grandfather always taught me, as the great-granddaughter of the late Emmett Lee King, that education was one of the most important aspects of life, one that no man can take away from me. I kept those words near and dear to my heart any time life presented me with a challenge.

My first career after obtaining my bachelor degree in May 2015 was rewarding and challenging at the same time; I had interned for a company two summers prior and received a job offer to work there after graduation. Due to my awesome internship experience, I was familiar with the dynamics of the business. I felt prepared to take on the opportunities to come and I knew I was destined for greatness. I enjoyed my customers, my associates, and the relationships I developed with other managers and supervisors. Halfway into my job, I started to think that there was something more to life, that I wanted and desired more. As this flame started to burn in my soul, I started to take an inventory of what I loved the most about my job, and how I could maximize the thing I loved and transform it into a career. I evaluated my life to see what my strengths and likes were, personally and professionally. I asked myself questions like: What part of my life was fulfilling? Can I make a career out of it? Were there opportunities for me to increase my knowledge in the subject matter? The most important question to me was, is this the calling on my life that God has for me? I realized that I loved empowering, challenging, growing, and molding individuals. This self-searching required some listening and waiting for the answers, and afterward seeking guidance from my mentors.

I started to research graduate schools and decided to apply to three programs. Throughout this process, I studied to prepare for the graduate admission test and decided to intentionally allow my faith and God to work on my behalf. I prayed at work at the same place and around the same time every day. My prayer was simple: "God, whatever you want me to do, I will do; wherever you want me to go, I will go." This prayer gave me peace and confidence, knowing that God was going to take me to a place that I wouldn't be able to reach by myself.

In November of 2015, my manager and I had a performance one-on-one. He asked me what it was that I wanted to do, and my response was human resources. He was discouraging and expressed to me that it would take me ten years to enter into that industry. He also stated that he didn't know how long I would continue to be an employee of the company, due to my failing numbers in a department that I did not know I was overseeing and had no training on. I was hurt. I wanted to quit, and I cried in my car on my lunch break. It took everything in me not to drive out of the parking lot and not return to my shift. I was determined, though, to not have to wait ten years to get into the industry that I had grown to love. I could not and did not allow that burning desire to die.

I prayed more, planned, and prepared, and in December 2015, Christmas came early; I received two letters of rejection, but also one letter of acceptance into graduate school. The one school I got accepted into was the one that would challenge me the most, spiritually, mentally, financially, and emotionally, which was all that I desired and prayed for. I decided to put the flame in me, one for pursuing training and development, to a test, and created a performance program that would both allow my numbers to improve and develop my associates along the way. I connected with colleagues throughout the company to help me gain insights on program implementation and sought their feedback on the program. This program became my passion. This program gave me purpose. I immersed myself into finding ways to strategically train, educate, motivate, and empower my associates.

As the numbers of my department started to increase, my dismissive manager was relocated to another store, and new leadership entered the store. As the new leadership transitioned, some of my of my associates started to receive recognition for having the best numbers in the district; it was confirmation that I was on my way to operating within the purpose God had for me.

Under new leadership, I continued to operate my program and sought to figure out where I would go for my next career move, or if my next career move would be within the company. One day, my new manager came and explained to me that the district manager wanted to put me on a performance plan because of my lack of performance. My manager gave me another option as well, which was to work in one of our makeup stores to improve my skills, since I loved makeup, and gave me three days to think about it.

As I left work that day, I was distraught yet determined once again. Distraught because that was not how I wanted to end my career with the company, but determined because I was already en route to accepting a scholarship that would help alleviate the cost of my graduate studies, meaning that keeping the job was no longer vital. On my first day off, I operated in a spirit of worry; on my second day off, I operated in a spirit of bitterness; but on the third day off, I decided that I would operate in a spirit of faith and resign from that job. I decided that I would take the time to prepare for graduate school, rest, and enjoy my time left in the South. It was a decision that no one saw coming, but because of my listening to God, I was able to take the right steps at the right time and trust that everything would work in my favor. Man gave me two options, but on the third day God revealed another option. I prepared for graduate school and moved from the south of the United States to the west to start a new life and a new graduate program; as I began the program, it was really rewarding and confirmed that the industry of human resources was for me. I had the support of my friends and family and I was excelling in the program and operating in the industry that I loved.

During my program, I decided to join a certain club, and I was nominated as vice president of the club. As vice president, I was to support the president in all initiatives and work together with them to get the club up and running successfully. I started to propose ideas and share ways I could help, but I noticed that my ideas were always rejected and I was always being undermined. I went from being a really eager vice president to a bitter one. In meetings, instead of making suggestions or proposing ideas, I learned to be quiet and observe the room; I started to watch the dynamics of the room and pay attention to the body language of the individuals there. I observed who was talking and agreeing with one another. I became frustrated; why was my voice being silenced, why was my voice being suppressed, why was everything I said undermined? I couldn't figure out why and it was painful. I would go to my room after meetings and cry; I would feel my heart beat so fast that it felt like it would explode; I would be tired, fatigued, and drained all at the same time. I just wanted my flame again, and I wanted my voice to be heard.

Christmas break came and I had no desire to return to the program. I wanted to quit so badly, but thankfully I have a village that doesn't allow me to give up and forces me to face the things that scare me the most. After returning from my Christmas break, God and I had a talk; we decided that I was going to maintain peace—and if something cost me my peace, it was too expensive. Maintaining peace reignited the flame in me; I would not allow the experience to break me, but instead to build me up, and I had to take the necessary steps to gain peace, share peace, protect my peace, and live in peace. I took the steps to live in peace and resigned as vice president of that club and instead partnered with other students to co-chair the business school's first diversity week. I became the media representative for the diversity week, and after the experience of being forced to be silent, my igniting flame and love for diversity and inclusion shone through. Diversity week was very impactful; I left each program feeling fulfilled, rewarded, and I connected with individuals who appreciated the safe space that was created there where people could be vulnerable.

The reality was that the role of vice president wasn't for me; God didn't ordain that, my name wasn't on that seat. I was to be in a different place, serving in my purpose in a different capacity. My purpose was to not only promote diversity and inclusion, but to give a voice to those who feel as though they have no voice. Diversity is the state of having a variety of cultures, skill sets, ideas, mentalities, and backgrounds. Inclusion is the state of listening and finding ways to implement those multifaceted ideas, skill sets, mentalities, and backgrounds into goals or initiatives that help a department or company achieve their overall strategy.

Life will be full of twists and turns. Do not be afraid to seek advice, ask questions, or speak up. Know that God hears your prayers; take the time to be still to listen to His answer. It is imperative to forgive others and yourself. As Romans 8:28 states, "and we know that in all things God works for the good of those who love him, who have been called according to His purpose" (NIV).

As for me, I know it is not enough to just have a seat at the table; my desires consist of making changes and having influence at the table. I want to be able to use the wisdom, skills, knowledge, and experience that God has given me to help inspire and ignite the people I work with to reach their goal or achieve their strategy. I didn't allow bitterness to block my blessings. I did not allow suppression to suffocate me. I had to transform my discomfort into determination, my fear into faith, and my pain into peace, and to use my voice to ignite victory.

I had to remind myself that I was the granddaughter of Emmett Lee King! I was created, covered, carried and crowned by the King, and it was time to awaken this world with the passion and purpose that God has given me.

Don't Fail to Gain Your Fortune

Bobby L. Tinnion

> "But I have prayed for you, Simon, that your faith may not fail. And when you have turned back, strengthen your brothers."
>
> —*Luke 22:32*

Many of us succeed in the common goal of attaining the highest levels of education with the highest of honors, yet, after completion of the educational process, end up failing in this thing called life. We achieve cum laude, magna cum laude, or even summa cum laude, but then become masters of "someone help me lawdy!" Life has its way of teaching us lessons that are either rarely or not at all taught in our educational institutions. These lessons are learned by most of the ordinary people in the world who have endured its calamities. We must become independent and empowered by being ahead of the vultures in society that ruin our generation by molding us to 1) graduate with college degrees, 2) work a forty hour per week job for forty years, laboring to pay back those expensive student loans, and then 3) retire broke and disillusioned. The vultures are the institutions—colleges, technical schools, universities, business merchants, and even governments—that ritualistically teach us, take our money, and then throw us into society not having a clue on how to advance within our learned fields.

With this chapter, it is my intention to aid ordinary people, equipping them with the Fs—faith, finance, family and fortune—on their report card of life to ultimately become extraordinary beings. I, too, have been faced with these very challenges and have learned to execute these Fs on my road to fortune and a bright future. Colloquial language is utilized throughout each F so that all of us, regardless of education level, might be able to attain the goals in life that have seemed, thus far, to only be available to the elite persons in our society.

FAITH—The first F is faith. The Holy Scripture tells us in Hebrews 11:6 that "without faith it is impossible to please him [God]: for he that comes to God must [first] believe that he is, and that he is a rewarder of them that diligently [persistently] seek him." It also states in Hebrews 11:1 that "faith is the substance of things hoped for, the evidence of things not seen." It is hard to accomplish even the smallest of any goals if one lacks faith. If one does not believe that he or she can do whatever plan and/or goal that has been set, it is not advisable for that individual to move forward with that plan. Faith is the eyeball of our minds, being able to see the end clearly, even before it has been accomplished. In other words, every person must intentionally begin his mission or plan with a thorough vision.

Throughout our modern times, there are a myriad of individuals who graduate from higher education without a tangible plan to be successful in life. Without a plan, it is like navigating a dark room you have never been in before or walking through life wearing a blindfold. One takes his steps carefully, but never knows which direction he is going, nor where or how his walk will end. I vividly recall my dream when entering into undergraduate school, pursuing my bachelor's degree. I said to my inner self, "I'm going to graduate, get me a good job, become wealthy, get married, start a family, buy my parents a new home, and then retire happy and healthy." As things turned out, I graduated, I got married, I have a job, I have a family, but that house for the parents, the wealth, and the retiring happy and healthy have taken on a totally new meaning. Life got a hold of me after graduating, and I found myself caught without a solid plan in place, which in turn shook my faith. I was lost and could only ask myself, "What do I do now, with no plan and a very shaky faith?"

I reached out to a couple of mentors, as well as a spiritual leader who had accomplished the things that I sought for myself. It turns out that all of my desires for success, morally and spiritually, were generic in nature. Like most of us, I wanted great things in life, but did not realize that a specific plan of action, along with a solid faith, were essential if I ever wanted to accomplish anything. When I asked the spiritual leader what I was doing wrong, He replied: you must have faith, first of all in yourself, and equally in God, who makes it all possible. I discovered that I was not as spiritually sound as I had perceived myself to be. My mentors answered in a similar fashion when I asked them what I was doing wrong and what I needed to do to advance forward. To my surprise, they replied by saying: you have to take care of you first. I concluded that I was (and in many cases still am) taking care of others rather than myself. Once the needs of others were met by me, I would then come home and realize that my own nest was lacking. These actions again shook my faith. After I was able to extract information from these experts and go into some deep meditation, I could see at once that it was time to turn things around immediately. I put my faith and future, spiritually and morally, in writing and started to take care of me, while not leaving others out. A periodical and proverbial look in the mirror at yourself is advised and warranted for every individual; you must tell the person in the mirror: "I can and I will!" Now, go look in the mirror at yourself and say to the person you see there: I have FAITH, and no one and nothing is going to shake it! I made my first F, my faith is strong, and I am proud of it!

FINANCE—Once you score the first F on your life's report card, it is now time for the second F, which is finance. You will now have to fund that plan that you spent countless hours of education, dedication, and meditation on while planning in your faith stage. In other words, it is time to get a job. This is a very important F. Most college graduates in the United States, once they have become gainfully employed, go to the already-successful merchants and financial institutions and borrow more money. This results in an overwhelming amount of debt that takes them their forty years of postgraduate time to pay back—then they turn sixty-two years old and attempt to survive off of our government's unstable social security contribution. This may seem awkward and unorthodox, or maybe even un-American, to many, but how about taking care of GOD and YOU FIRST? Taking out unnecessary loans and buying unnecessary things only makes the rich richer. I learned this concept from the financial mentors and advisors that came into my life when I was middle-aged. Of course, at the time of being educated by these mentors, I had already taken out loans and was already doing my ritual of making the rich richer. When I implemented the "take care of you first" attitude, it still took me some time to gain control of the concept and move forward. I created a budget and I stick to it religiously. At every pay period, set aside a minimum of ten percent for God and for you, first, resulting in about twenty percent of your earnings! The remaining eighty percent goes to everyone and everything else.

The question for most of us is: how are you going to manage to save ten percent for yourself, give God at least ten percent, and still survive off the remaining eighty percent? I am glad you asked. I have a question for you: Who told you that you only had to work forty hours in a week? One of the key elements with and common denominators for most successful people is hard work. No laws, rules, or regulations demand that one is limited to a forty-hour workweek. It is imperative to work as much as you need to achieve the goals that you've set for your future fortune. I know it doesn't sit well with the general public to see a corporate executive working a part-time job at a fast food restaurant, but if the F plan is followed and consistently executed, we will see who is laughing in the end. Let's look at an example of that saving ten percent concept: At a salary of one thousand dollars per week, ten percent would be one hundred dollars per week. That, times fifty-two weeks a year at twelve percent interest annually would equal approximately one million dollars in just over twenty-five years. If someone started right out of college (average age is early to mid-twenties), one would become a millionaire by the time he or she is fifty years old. How would you like to retire with one million dollars before reaching the age of sixty-two? I made the second F, my finances are solid, and I am proud of it!

FAMILY—After one has aligned and accomplished his or her FAITH and FINANCES, the next major step toward a successful journey is developing the family. This step can make or break the two previous grades. First, it is important to choose a life partner or spouse that is on board with your faith and who will not drain your financial plans and goals.

When the vow "until death do us part" is professed in the eyes of God and witnesses, there is no turning back. While spending time dating potential candidates, make a list of ten items that you will not compromise on in a relationship. The first item should be a spouse that will not interfere with your faith and the second should be a spouse that will not interfere with your finances, instead having a clear vision of a successful future. I am not a licensed relationship counselor, but I feel dating should not be taken lightly. Thus, if your potential spouse or the person you date happens to be a heavy spender and has no regard for his or her posterity, he or she will most likely not change that habit during a committed lifetime relationship. This is only one out of your ten, but it could prove fatal in a relationship if not regarded before making a decision. Always remember that habits are difficult to make, but they are equally difficult to break.

Family has always been my toughest assignment on my journey. I never wanted to rely on anyone to take care of them and I take great pride in doing so on my own. But from the countless hours of commitment to work throughout my career, I missed many greater opportunities. The glory of it is that my family, my wife and daughter, knew and understood why I did it and they were on board with my plan, even when it was failing at the time. Because we are a tightly bonded family, they support me and I am eternally grateful for them. The household bond is strong, our spirit and faith are strong, and my daughter has made great strides in her educational, family, and financial life. I was not able to write this segment about success and fortune with a dry eye because of the support my family has offered me. I cannot reiterate enough how important it is to date dutifully and choose the right candidate as a life partner for the development of your family. I made my third F: my family is sound and I am proud of it!

FORTUNE—If you are in your college years, it is time to carefully consider your life action plan of faith, family, finances, and, ultimately, fortune. Conversely, if you are a seasoned adult, already in the midst of the storm of life, it is time to carefully consider a change of attitude and start implementing these Fs in your life. It is never too late to begin, but it must start with you. I was always told in my manufacturing years that if you do the same thing, you'll get the same results. Later, in my ministerial experience, I heard it said in a slightly different way: if nothing changes, nothing changes. In other words, if your life is stuck on a treadmill and doesn't seem to be advancing as you had planned, it is time to change your plan.

Whatever you do, do not ever allow your faith to fail, finances to falter, family not to be fed, or your fortune to be frazzled. Stay physically and spiritually fit and you will be on your way to a bright and productive future. Strive for that inner peace that passes all understanding, making our fellow citizens wonder why you are in your condition. Show the world how you have been transformed with a renewed mind and spirit. Then, equip them with the ultimate knowledge of how you got there. I am on a clear path toward accomplishing my final F; my future and fortune awaits me and appears attainable before reaching the governmental age of sixty-two, not having to rely solely on Social Security benefits, and I am proud of it! Why are you still reading this story? Get motivated and go and get your fortune! I hope you make straight Fs on your life's report card.

Living My Purpose—Finance and Entrepreneurship

Kawana L. Marshall

"Bring ye all the tithes into the storehouse, that there may be meat in mine house, and prove me now herewith, saith the Lord of hosts, if I will not open you the windows of heaven, and pour you out a blessing, that there shall not be room enough to receive it."

—*Malachi 3:10*

In the era of social media, we tend to spotlight the Yves Saint Laurent® side of our lives while camouflaging our Faded Glory® side. Many of us never mention the journey until we are speaking of the victory. However, the journey is just as important as the victory. The process of achieving success is the most valuable part of the experience because it is the learning and development phase that ultimately propels us to greatness. Specifically, for me, I embraced my journey, as I have gained a tremendous amount of priceless information, both through trial and error and from the assistance of mentors, family, and friends. Therefore, as a small business consultant, I am able to provide both theoretical and practical knowledge to my clients and other budding entrepreneurs. As an entrepreneur with both successes and many failures, however, my journey continues.

From an early age, I knew that I wanted to become an entrepreneur, but I didn't know how or where to start. I only knew that I wanted to own a business, employ family members, and have the financial freedom to own multiple homes and cars and to travel the world. My mother can attest to the fact that I resisted learning how to cook because my plan was always to have a personal chef. My husband and I have been together for over a decade and he still complains about my cooking skills. The desire to become an entrepreneur was always a thought for me, but I initially suppressed it due to fear of the unknown.

Entrepreneurship is not only about a creative, innovative, or technological idea, it is also about business. If you are familiar with the TV show Shark Tank, the sharks always ask the entrepreneurs to tell them about their business revenues, valuations, customer acquisition, etc. At the core of every business is capital. Capital in the terms of money, credit, and overall finances. Every business requires some form of a capital investment in order to open its doors and to maintain. Since an entrepreneur starts most small businesses from scratch, I knew that it was imperative for me to have somewhat of a solid understanding of both business and personal finances to succeed. Personal finances can be a deal breaker when it comes to starting a business. For one, it takes capital to properly organize a business. There are fees that must be paid to the secretary of state, and in some jurisdictions, there are fees that must be paid to the local municipalities. Depending on the nature of your business, there are expenses for office space, supplies, marketing, advertising, accounting, and even labor. All of these things were very intimidating to me, which delayed and deterred my aspirations of entrepreneurship. In addition, I was afraid to fail. After researching the journey of other entrepreneurs, failure usually seemed to occur before any success was reached. However, after having two children and getting married, I finally decided to take that leap into entrepreneurship.

I initially started my first business in 2008 while still working in corporate America. Although I did not technically work on my business while on the job, I did spend a significant amount of my downtime writing and formulating my ideas while on breaks. Additionally, whenever I had time in between working, I would make phone calls or send emails from my mobile phone to potential customers. Nonetheless, the income I received from my job provided the necessary capital investment for my husband and I to build our first business. Although working a full-time job while trying to start a business is not the most productive use of your time, it does provide a security net while growing your business. Because I was a mother of two, I relied heavily on my job for medical benefits and secondary income. Making the decision to leave my job was one of the most difficult decisions that I have ever made in my life. At the time, I had a very secure job within the pharmaceutical industry. In my hometown, it was considered one of the best companies to work for in the area. In making the decision, I had to consider not only myself, but also my children. As a mother, I wanted to be a role model for my children and provide a life for them in which they had an abundance of choices. So late in 2011, I made the leap of faith and put in my resignation. The last two weeks on my job were immensely stressful, as I had worked continuously up until that point since the age of sixteen. My husband was already full-time in the business, so that meant that the business would be the ONLY source of income for the entire family. However, we put our faith in God and continued the course.

In addition to the capital, credit was essential in order for us to secure a bond for our business at an affordable rate. I knew that building and maintaining a good credit score was imperative for our business finances as well as our personal finances. One important way that I learned to build good credit is to always have a budget. Budgeting is the most effective tool for managing your money. With a budget, you are able to preplan what you can afford and eliminate or reduce expenses where possible. For instance, one quick way to reduce your monthly expenses is to increase your car insurance deductible. With car insurance, you essentially pay a premium to have a $250 or $500 deductible. Another quick and easy win is through bundling services with one service provider.

Although reducing expenses is an effective way to build credit by way of savings, it is equally important to always pay all bills on time. There is generally a thirty-day window allowed starting from the billing date to pay bills without risk of the late payment being reported to the credit bureaus. However, as a rule of thumb, you should always pay your bills on or before the due date to avoid the added late fees. Late fees are detrimental to any budget and overall financial plan. The money that we spend on late fees can be invested into a 401(k), IRA, or other savings vehicle.

Monitoring your credit is just as important as building good credit. It is always a good idea to know your credit score. Many services on the market offer credit monitoring. However, when selecting a credit monitoring service, it is necessary to read the fine print. Some credit monitoring services provide you with free credit scores, but come with the hidden agenda of selling your personal and credit information to third parties. The third parties in turn begin to send you offers for credit cards, auto-financing, and other products. For years, I only used myfico.com to monitor my credit; now my bank offers free credit monitoring. As a business owner, with no other source of income, I studied money and finances daily, when I could, or as often as possible to increase my awareness and armor myself with the tools to succeed.

Our finances are vital to every aspect of our lives, including gaining access to quality healthcare, qualifying for a mortgage or even rent, getting reasonable terms on auto-financing, and more. Without a holistic understanding of the financial landscape, you may not be able to realize what is known as the American Dream.

In the early stages of my adulthood, I wasn't focused on the American Dream or saving for my future. I was only focused on the NOW. I was focused on enjoying my money that day and that week. Personally, I have made some absurdly poor financial decisions in my life; however, those poor decisions are a part of my testimony and experience that I can share with various audiences. Although it is essential that we enjoy the now, while enjoying the now we must also intentionally plan. Planning includes creating a financial portfolio to help secure your financial success. It is a myth that you have to be rich to have a financial or investment portfolio. You can start your investment portfolio with a relatively small sum of money because there are many investment options on the market. You can invest in your own business or invest in an external business. You can invest in your job's 401(k) plan as well as a traditional or Roth IRA. In addition, you can invest in stocks, municipal bonds, or federal bonds. Again, you can invest in so many ways. The objective is to save and to invest in something that is conducive to your overall financial plan. My business is one of my main investments. Additionally, I maintain a savings account and a couple CDs with my bank; however, I soon learned that was not enough. Through research and formal training, I learned that the most advantageous savings strategy is having a mix of aggressive and conservative investments that have significant tax advantages. As an IRS-enrolled agent, I always consider the tax implications of investments and savings. Having both pretax and after-tax investments in your portfolio is heavily advised.

Currently, I have focused my career on providing financial, tax planning, and investment advice to my clients and others. I made it my mission to educate our clients on how to break the cycle of debt and how to build wealth. To ensure that I provide the most reliable and comprehensive advice to my clients, I continued my education and became licensed to sell annuities, insurance, and investments. In addition, the knowledge and advice that I share has been acquired through many years of formal education, career experience, and life experience. I remind everyone that they can have financial freedom with discipline and hard work. The hard work may include having multiple jobs at one time and/or starting a business. Although entrepreneurship has significant risks, it can also be more rewarding than a traditional career or job. Discipline, however, includes reducing unnecessary spending and minimizing or eliminating credit card debt. Credit card debt is one of the worst forms of debt, as it typically has the highest interest rates. Although it is advised to have at least one credit card for emergencies as well as for your overall credit mix, credit cards should only be utilized with extreme discretion. Credit cards can help build your credit, but they can also have adverse consequences when maxed out. Trust me, I know personally.

In the earlier stages of my entrepreneurial journey, I encountered many obstacles. One of the main obstacles was deciding on the most optimal location for my business. This was one of the greatest pain points for me, as well as many other entrepreneurs. Location, location, location, as many of us have heard, can sometimes determine whether or not your business fails or succeeds. This does not hold true for all businesses, but it is critical for most. My initial business model was to provide accounting and tax preparation services for a wide range of clients. I wanted to provide services for business owners as well as the working class. However, early on I was advised that the low- to middle-income class was more concerned about the end product than the location. As long as I could legally reduce their tax liability and/or get the largest refund, the working class clients would patronize my business. However, there are some upper middle class clients and business owners that expect a location in an affluent business district. So, in the beginning, I decided on what I had discovered was an underserved area. The area was modest, spacious, and, most importantly, within my budget. However, although it was within my personal budget, I failed to consider my business budget. I learned from experience that it is of the utmost importance to create a business budget. The business budget, which serves as an overarching guide, is your financial plan of projected revenues and expenses for the year. When you create a business budget, you can measure how your business is performing month after month. Tracking and measuring your financial performance provides guidance for decision-making. Decisions such as whether or not to reallocate funds or increase your personal investment into the business should only be considered once you have reviewed and analyzed your business budget. Today, I live by budgets.

Another obstacle early in my business was the absence or lack of policies, procedures, and internal controls. In order for me to provide consistent, reliable service to clients, policies and procedures had to be developed and standardized. For me, I had to develop policies and procedures for everything, from filing documents to printing checks. Concurrently, I also had to develop internal controls to ensure those policies were executed as necessary by myself as well as by my partner and assistants. Of course, access to certain functions were restricted due to the sensitivity of the information handled at my office.

In addition to obstacles, I also learned some critical lessons. To date, the biggest lessons that I have learned is to ALWAYS back up system data on an external hard drive. In year one of my business, midway through my busy season, I had a major system failure and lost all of the electronic copies of a majority of my clients' information. I was so devastated and could not believe that my new computer system crashed. Although the system would periodically signal for me to back up data, I would bypass the message and continue working. At that time, I figured that as it was a new computer with plenty of storage, I would just back it up later. Well, lesson learned. I spent hundreds of dollars in an attempt to recover the data, but was grossly unsuccessful. From that day forward, I set up my computer system to automatically back up the data every day to an external hard drive. Additionally, I periodically back up the external hard drive to another hard drive to provide that extra layer of security.

Entrepreneurship is a journey. It is not something that you master on day one, month one, or even year one. In order to become successful, you must commit to continuous learning and development, along with continuous investment in your business. The business plan must also be revised to reflect new developments in your business, in the industry, or in technology in general. As technology in your industry changes, so must your business. Each year, I attend live trainings, webinars, and continuing education classes to remain current with the ever-changing regulations and trends in my industry.

As a serial entrepreneur, I personally encourage anyone that has a passion or dream to pursue it. I also highly recommend for any aspiring entrepreneur to seek out mentors. Mentors can assist with navigating the unknown and reducing the learning curve. Mentors also provide insight on their past experiences and knowledge gained through years of experience. If you are considering entrepreneurship, create your plan, meditate on it, and seek guidance from the Almighty.

All in all, I have definitely learned from all the poor financial decisions that I made in my lifetime, from acquiring excessive student loan debt to overspending on designer brands and lavish vacations. As my mother would tell me, "When you know better, you do better," and I am definitely doing better by making wiser financial decisions while helping others along the way.

Sources

Baer, Drake. 2013. "Why Openness to Experience Is the Key to Creativity." *Fast Company*, December 4. https://www.fastcompany.com/3022490/why-openness-to-experience-is-the-key-to-creativity.

Bronson, Po, and Ashley Merryman. 2010. "The Creativity Crisis." *Newsweek*, July 10. http://www.newsweek.com/2010/07/10/the-creativity-crisis.html.

Fiske, Edward B. 2002. "Learning in Deed: The Power of Service-Learning for American Schools." National Commission on Service-Learning.

Merisotis, Jamie P. 2013. "Quality Education in the Global Context: What We Are All Learning about Learning." Speech, AHELO Conference, Paris, France, March 11. Lumina Foundation. https://www.luminafoundation.org/news-and-views/quality-education-in-the-global-context-what-we-are-all-learning-about-learning.

Ng, A. S., and K. Kaye. 2012. "Why It Matters: Teen Childbearing, Education, and Economic Wellbeing." Washington, DC: The National Campaign to Prevent Teen and Unplanned Pregnancy.

Sources

Unless otherwise indicated, scripture quotations are from the Holy Bible, King James Version. All rights reserved.

Scriptures marked AMP are taken from the Amplified Version®. Copyright © 2015 by The Lockman Foundation. All rights reserved.

Scriptures marked NIV are taken from the New International Version®. Copyright © 1973, 1978, 1984, 2011 by Biblica, Inc.™. All rights reserved.

Scriptures marked NKJV are taken from the New King James Version®. Copyright © 1982 by Thomas Nelson. All rights reserved.

WhiteSpace at Work. 2018. http://www.whitespaceatwork.com

Wujec, Tom. 2010. "Build a Tower, Build a Team." Filmed February 2010. TED video. https://www.ted.com/talks/tom_wujec_build_a_tower?language=en

About the Authors

JaTaun Hawkins

JaTaun Hawkins is a two-time cancer survivor whose passion is helping women find their strength in broken places. Through her own struggles with divorce, bankruptcy, broken engagements, and a life-threatening illness, JaTaun learned to embrace her own worth and guide others toward a vibrant, free, and abundant life.

JaTaun learned the power of hard work through her twenty-two years in the automotive finance industry and her interior decorating business, Touch of Claassy Production. She serves the community through Girl Scout leadership and groups like Yannasisters, Curlfriends Abroad, Black Girls Swing, and Girl Talk Dallas. She also enjoys international travel and spending time with her four beautiful grandchildren.

A native New Yorker, JaTaun now lives outside Dallas, Texas. In 2018 she'll be cohosting a TV travel show, "The Ultimate Experience Abroad," and publishing her first book,

I Didn't Know My Own Strength.

Connect with JaTaun at www.jataunhawkins.com

Patrice Withers-Stephens

Patrice Withers-Stephens is a talented professional with over twelve years of experience in nonprofit management, corporate responsibility and reputation, communications, and public relations. Patrice is a summa cum laude graduate of North Carolina A&T State University, where she received a bachelor of science degree in journalism and mass communication with a concentration in public relations. She also holds a master of arts in professional development from Amberton University.

Her greatest passion is to serve those with the greatest needs. Most recently, Women of Visionary Influence, Incorporated, recognized her as a Mentor of the Year Finalist for the Nonprofit Sector. She is a member of the Potter's House of North Dallas and the Alpha Kappa Alpha Sorority, Incorporated®, as well as a founding board member of Bridge2Greatness, Incorporated.

After residing in the great state of Texas for twelve years, she finally considers north Texas home, though she will never depart from her North Carolina roots.

Learn more at: https://pnwspeaks.wordpress.com/

Tiffany D. Hicks

Tiffany D. Hicks is a consultant, coach, facilitator, and writer. Born in the south suburbs of Chicago, Tiffany was raised in western New York and currently resides in the Dallas/Fort Worth area.

Having graduated with a bachelor of science in technical management, Tiffany has worked most of her professional career at a Fortune 100 company, where she holds an assistant vice president title. Her professional aptitudes include speaking, training, leader development and performance improvement, process design, and program and project management at a corporate level. She has a passion for helping others and is a believer in the principles of servant leadership.

In addition to her work, Tiffany has a deep love for her family and enjoys traveling, reading, enjoying literary and performing arts, and tapping into her artistic side via painting and crafting.

Connect with Tiffany at JustTiffany517@gmail.com

Brigid Roberson

Brigid Roberson is a mentor, corporate executive, and motivational speaker who believes in helping others achieve their dreams and goals. She is the CEO and Founder of Bridge2Greatness, Incorporated, a 501 (c) (3) nonprofit designed to provide resources and mentoring opportunities for at-risk girls. Brigid is an ambitious doctoral student of Interdisciplinary Leadership with a master's in executive management and a bachelor's in communications. She has led large organizations through crisis and triumph. She requires the same for herself, pushing through to victory despite obstacles and her meek upbringing. She is an avid philanthropist devoted to achieving greatness by carving out a unique "servant leadership" niche, building others up, illuminating positivity, and maximizing people's full potential.

Brigid's mission in life is dedicated to empowering girls and women, leading by example, and mentoring. She is committed to life-long learning and believes that everyone has greatness inside that is waiting to be unleashed.

Learn more at www.bridge2greatness.com

LaTisha Terry

LaTisha Terry currently serves in a leadership role within the financial industry. She has been helping people in this capacity over the last ten years. Her career has afforded her many opportunities to lead others to reach their career and personal goals. LaTisha pursued a major in communications at Alabama A&M University, where she earned her bachelor of arts degree in 2006. She also obtained her master of business administration degree from Cardinal Stritch University in 2010. LaTisha is a native of Milwaukee, Wisconsin, and currently residing in Dallas, Texas.

LaTisha is also the founder of Fancy Chat. Fancy Chat is here to keep you financially sound, provide knowledge, and empower you to be the very best you! The information provided by Fancy Chat expands to other topics as well, such as the natural hair movement and how to live a healthy lifestyle, to name a few.

Learn more at www.fancychatblog.com

Floyd Dorsey IV

Floyd Dorsey IV is a natural motivator and influencer; however, those characteristics did not come easy. He attributes both his personal and professional achievements to his innate realization of the best in every individual and situation. He has moved from his beginnings in small town Tyler, Texas, to achieve many successes, yet has remained humble. His time on the field as a football player ignited his drive, focus, and dedication. He gives back intentionally with the same passion.

Floyd is the true essence of a Renaissance Man. As a leader in corporate America, he continues to influence significant operational improvements for various organizations. Beyond his professional career, he offers motivational talks geared toward encouraging positive thought and strategic action. Floyd's consistent positive energy and confidence always piques the interest of audiences.

Floyd is dedicated to building next generation leaders, leveraging his personal motto "Think—Do—Be—Do—Have™."

Connect with Floyd at support@IVTuneEnterprise.com

Dr. Tara Peters

Dr. Tara Peters is a gifted educator who believes there is no greater calling than educating our future generations. A professional educator for more than twenty-four years, she currently serves as academic dean for the Texas campus of Northwood University and professor in the DeVos Graduate School. She earned a PhD in educational leadership and systems and has been invited to teach on multiple occasions in Northwood's international programs. She consults internationally and her scholarly work has been presented at regional and national conferences. Dr. Peters coauthored "The Underrepresentation of African American Women in Executive Leadership: What's Getting in the Way." She's been recognized for excellence in the classroom by Who's Who Among America's Teachers and administrative excellence as a National Woman's History Month honoree. In her leisure, she loves to travel the world and has visited twenty-seven countries. She's the proud mother of an attorney and aspiring entrepreneur, Generra.

Learn more at www.drtarapeters.com

T'Edra Z. Jackson

T'Edra Z. Jackson, MS, is a Baton Rouge, Louisiana, native. She received her bachelor of science in business administration management from Paul Quinn College. She completed her master of science in human resources from Pepperdine University. She recently launched her blog Kingsskid, where she strives to educate individuals on how God creates, covers, carries, and crowns them, working through personal, professional, and mentor-mentee development. When she isn't reading, she is blogging, cooking, traveling, and mentoring young ladies.

Connect with T'Edra at www.kingsskid.com

Bobby L. Tinnion

Bobby L. Tinnion is a man of many talents and great accomplishments. He is a giver by nature and has a heart dedicated to sharing God's word. Pouring into others is woven into the fabric of his being.

Growing up in the southern sector of Dallas, Texas, Bobby developed a deep passion for helping others within underserved communities. As a result of his passion, he continues to mentor and sponsor individuals, which led to his progression in ministry. As a minister, Bobby is committed to introducing others to God and offering messages backed by biblical evidence. He shares spirit-filled messages at his congregation and also spreads the word at other congregations and in the community.

Bobby sings with the Dallas Opera and established Christian Apparel Company in 2000, a company designed to personalize apparel for special events. Amidst all successes, his greatest joy is his wife and daughter.

Learn more at www.christianapparelco.com

Kawana L. Marshall

Kawana L. Marshall, a native of Gloster, Louisiana, is a wife and mother of two handsome, intelligent sons. She is also the owner of Infinity Tax and Accounting, Inc., a boutique accounting firm with offices in Shreveport, Louisiana, and Dallas, Texas. In addition to her accounting career, Kawana and her husband also operate a transportation company.

Kawana is a graduate of Louisiana State University–Shreveport and Texas A&M–Commerce, with a bachelor of science degree in accounting and an MBA in finance. Her civic and community ties are extensive and include affiliation or membership in several notable organizations, including the Sigma Rho Omega chapter of Alpha Kappa Alpha Sorority, Incorporated, Order of Eastern Star, Shreveport Bossier African American Chamber of Commerce, and Junior League of Dallas.

When time permits, Kawana enjoys traveling the world and honing her skills in financial planning and real estate investing.

Learn more at http://www.itaaccounting.com/

Dr. Jatun Dorsey

Dr. Jatun Dorsey is a professional speaker, life and business coach, professor, author, and corporate leader. With a doctorate in business administration and certifications in dispute resolution and coaching, she strives to help people who are launching or enhancing a business to maintain a work-life balance. She does this by teaching them how to manage their time in order to meet both the demands of their career and the passions of their heart in a stress-free environment.

Dr. Jatun is also the founder of The Commend Her Network, a nonprofit organization focused on partnering with local women's shelters to aid underprivileged girls and women in gaining confidence for facing life and reentering the workforce. When not focusing on her passion of inspiring and helping others, she enjoys spending time with her family, dancing, relaxing, and singing karaoke. Dr. Jatun lives in the Dallas, Texas metroplex with her husband.

To learn more, visit her website at www.drjatun.com

Visionary Author Connection

Dr. T. Jatun Dorsey,
CEO DrJatun.com and Founder/Executive Director of
The Commend Her Network (TCHN)

5729 Lebanon Rd
Ste.144-300
Frisco, TX 75034
469-609-7526

MEET ME ONLINE:

www.drjatun.com or Jatun@drjatun.com

www.commendhernetwork.org or
Jatun@commendhernetwork.org

CREATING DISTINCTIVE BOOKS WITH INTENTIONAL RESULTS

We're a collaborative group of creative masterminds with a mission to produce high-quality books to position you for monumental success in the marketplace.

Our professional team of writers, editors, designers, and marketing strategists work closely together to ensure that every detail of your book is a clear representation of the message in your writing.

Want to know more?
Write to us at info@publishyourgift.com
or call (888) 949-6228

Discover great books, exclusive offers, and more at
www.PublishYourGift.com

Connect with us on social media

@publishyourgift

www.ingramcontent.com/pod-product-compliance
Lightning Source LLC
Chambersburg PA
CBHW071519080526
44588CB00011B/1485